The Accidental Societist

How to build a fairer economy, politics and society

PETER ELLIS

Grosvenor House
Publishing Limited

This book is published by
Grosvenor House Publishing Ltd
Link House
140 The Broadway, Tolworth, Surrey, KT6 7HT.
www.grosvenorhousepublishing.co.uk

A CIP record for this book
is available from the British Library

ISBN 978-1-80381-784-2
eBook ISBN 978-1-80381-785-9

Cover art by Celeste Byers.
*Cover illustration, this artwork is reproduced with the kind permission of Celeste
Byers. Celeste created 'We Are American' in 2019* for Amplifier Foundation's
Realising Democracy project. *A full copy of this image is shown in
Appendix 2 – 'Realising Democracy/Celeste Byers artwork'.
(celestebyers.com/celestebyers@gmail.com)*

This book is dedicated to my partner Sarah,
who has encouraged me constantly to put pen to paper,
and to Kathryn and Alex; may you and the generations who
follow you build a better future based on values of justice,
fairness, and common well-being.

To the fellowship of those of us who seek greater economic
and social justice, to the politicians, entrepreneurs,
economists, and academics, those with the power
to enable reform, and to the students and young
people who will elect and govern in years to come.
Let us settle on a unique, ubiquitous, and
separate system, neither capitalist nor statist, which
operates for our common good, asserting the
political power and economics of society,
and societal best interest.

We can change society.

You are an individual with human, social and economic rights.
You are significant and will have your own personal beliefs and
values. You live in society, mutually dependent on others, with
personal talents, skills and self-understanding which promotes
your well-being and happiness, and those you live with in society.

You are a societal being.   As am I.

If you have any comments on or want to engage further with
ideas for societal reform then visit **thesocietyproject.org.uk** or
email **peter.ellis.society@gmail.com**.

Contents

Foreword

Often, I walk and notice how a child, independent from a parent in so many ways, walks similarly to that parent, the same gait, stride length and foot fall. As my daughter, son and I wander across fields and paths, I cannot deny that from behind, any casual viewer would see that we share inherited characteristics, walking in the steps of our forebears. More than that, we tread the same footpaths I walked as a boy, part of a heritable environment.

I long for my children to find their own way in life, free from the pre-conceived ideas I may have unintentionally planted in them, to travel their own, unique journey, unencumbered by tradition, and that they find ways of being and living that are relevant to their modern time, and that of their contemporaries; that they challenge the status quo previous generations, mine included, have bequeathed them, to build a better future.

That future is determined largely, as it is for all of us, by our collective inheritance, of an economic and political system underpinned by social and political philosophies that should be just and fair, that strengthen the ties that bind us together as a society with shared values, and allow us to live, however we choose, safely and secure in the provision of the essential elements of our lives, economic, human and environmental.

The legacy we have inherited, systems founded on hierarchy, ownership and control have led to a binary economic system which has a polarising reflection in our politics. This is not how it should be. We are a diverse society, individuals living side by side, with different, often conflicting views on every matter under the sun. For democracy to be fully representative, our politics and economy should be plural too, but neither is. To bequeath a more just economy we need to challenge this economic and political settlement.

Rudimental forces define our collective economic identity, they determine for many of us an experience of economic life disconnected from our personal values, a system whose parameters we unconsciously accept, the reality of which leaves us feeling disempowered.

We can be inspired on our journey of reform by vision. John Lennon's imaginings set us on our path in search of tolerance, civilising values, and justice. We travel the poet John Donne's river, which kisses one bank then does kiss the next, achieving the purest change. We should be moved by Steve McQueen's dramatic retelling of racial discrimination, and make the links of that lived experience, also suffered through gender and social class, to the cause of economic empowerment. At the end of our travel, we must leave the barren landscape which does not nourish and where too many are told they will not grow, to live in a new land that is fertile, where marigolds will bloom, with roots that persevere, and the marginalised and disadvantaged will have "power beyond measure", the vision of the poet Alissa Jacques. This is not then a matter purely of economics, it is about conceptual reformation. It is also of profound relevance to groups we refer to as minorities in this country, who may be global majorities, and to majorities, including women, who are disempowered; one cannot understate the importance of group action in the cause of economic reform.

Humanity faces existential and systemic challenges which can be a catalyst for positive change, encouraging the pursuit of universal values, common interest, sustainability, and sufficiency. Particularly for the global fellowship of reformers, but for the general population too, seeking change, we often face an economy that diminishes our society through unequal shares of wealth, opportunity, and outcome.

Our economy is driven by legacy, not the needs of a modern society. While society has evolved, our economy has not. To build an inclusive, well-being economy, with prosperity shared fairly requires a democratic economic system, one working for the collective good.

There are many positive achievements from commercial endeavour in the private sector, by shareholders seeking private gain: personal and social progress, economic growth, with trading surpluses generated, the tax on which has helped fund social and public expenditure. Through taxation and government's power to redistribute national wealth, a level of fairness ensures social cohesion is maintained. However, market capitalism is not fit, in its exclusivity, for societal purpose. It was never designed to serve social need as its primary function.

There is a distinction to be made between that part of the private sector in which individuals seek to make a living and prosper through a business they are employed in and perhaps own, and that part comprising companies having a wider societal impact, and relevance, owned by shareholders as capital investments, often remote from the day-to-day work of the companies in which they invest. It is that part of the private sector which this book concerns, the one defined as market capitalist. The monopoly which market capitalism enjoys over the free-market, and over the profits consumers generate through their demand, denies the general population a truly mixed and plural economy intrinsically serving their best interests.

The aim of this book is to answer the question, "if not capitalism, what"?

Private sector capitalism, rooted in hierarchy, patriarchy, control, and ownership, developed at a time of no universal franchise, no race or gender equality. Economic rights were held by a male, property-owning minority. Force, military power, and colonisation were the tools of private acquisition overseas. Little wonder Marxism (and the socialism that derived from it) demanded ownership pass to the workers and state.

Perhaps our notion of enterprise and economy would have changed as society evolved but for the trauma of the cold war. The late Dr Naomi Fisher wrote on behavioural genetics and psychology. She observed that our DNA makes us who we are, so attempts at change are limited by our personal experience and genes, and she observed that our genes and environment act in myriad, interconnected, heritable ways. Our economy is no different, as we accept a framework based on beliefs rooted in the past, seemingly unable to adapt as society changes. Meanwhile our daily transactions affect our consciousness and understanding of the economy in a behavioural and systemic loop. Our views become polarised, and we find it hard to imagine a for-profit enterprise economy, other than as a private sector one, shareholder owned, yet a societal economy exists already. We simply do not recognise it, and because we do not identify it, we do not develop its full potential.

A societised free market enterprise economy is one served by companies independent of shareholders or state; trust and societally purposed companies generating sufficient profit to sustain their business and not returning unretained profit to shareholders. Instead, using it for defined societal purposes. It is the embodiment of a sustainable and sufficient economy. A food retailer might increase profits to fund non-profit purposes helping charities eradicate food poverty. Or it might reduce profits to offer consumers in deprived areas lower food prices. Where would you choose to buy your weekly groceries from? Virtue-driven consumerism, with customers purchasing from companies whose purposes they believe in, attached to societally purposed enterprise, funded by social equity, democratises the economy. It passes power to individuals who might otherwise be disempowered or marginalised.

Personal well-being cannot be attained through unrelenting personal consumption, but virtue-consumption linked to societal purpose can advance our personal and societal well-being. This creates a framework for systemic change, building a a well-being economy through market societism. Consumer choice can determine economic outcomes not the maximisation of profit and shareholder interest. This is particularly important because equality, good mental health, the quality of our lived experience and societal life – indeed almost every aspect of our well-being is affected by our economy and the society it creates and influences.

Equality, living standards and outcome are determined by the way profit and economic purpose attach to pre-existing capital and wealth. The lines which divide society can be traced to the magnetic force which draws power and profit towards private capital, and in favour of those who already own it. A societal economy breaks the link between pre-existing capital and outcome, in favour of the general population.

We can be inspired by Motkraft in Norway, started by Bjorn Spieler and his fellow students. It is purposed to provide energy at cost for households, generating sufficient profit to sustain its business, and reduce the cost of living for its customers. The Patagonia group supply clothing. Yvon Chouinard, following his personal ethical values, decided to "go purpose", and structured the group as a benefit corporation through a trust and collective organisation, to use its profits to impact non-profit purpose, chiefly related to the environment. Patagonia is avowedly a societal company, for-profit, competitive in the free market, and using its profits for a societal purpose.

A societal sector can reduce the cost of living and provide a better deal for customers across the economy, but particularly where buyers form an identifiable group with similar requirements, such as for energy, water, and travel. It is suitable where there is pooling of risk, such as insurance. It can help achieve ethical outcomes related to business activity, and a greater representation of wider stakeholder interests. Staff connect as stakeholders in many ways, including when enterprises recognise purposeful employment contributes to personal well-being. Customers connect as stakeholders through consumer and societal benefit, but also through operating practices. The adoption of slow checkout lanes to combat loneliness in some societally purposed businesses, can be contrasted with the use of technology to remove staff in those seeking to maximise shareholders' returns.

Further, our public services will benefit from societisation. The emerging market for cannabis is one example. Societised production would give the NHS a supply for medicinal use at low prices, and profits from other legal sales could be used to counter the social costs of drug addiction. A societal response to the housing crisis, would compel us to use our existing housing stock, a national societal asset, to create affordable, societal market tenancies.

My journey to this point began when I founded an organisation advocating the use of our existing housing stock to create affordable, societal tenancies; "societising" the imperfect housing market. It was only later that

I thought I had better check to see if there was a philosophy that attaches to the values I ascribed to and underpins the societal economy, and I discovered an underdeveloped social philosophy called societism, a social philosophy 'that promotes the well-being of the group without sacrificing the significance of the individual'. I am therefore an accidental societist.

It is an exciting and hopeful prospect that through our imagination, ability, and ingenuity we can take a simple philosophical idea and build it into a meaningful cause for reform, founded on universal values rooted in our commonality.

We just need to connect the dots. Common values systems exist across national boundaries, and are shared by populations across the globe, the societal economy exists, it is just not identified and developed as such and there is a political mandate to serve the best interest of general populations and the societies they form. Long held, impactful capitalistic assumptions about how the mixed market economy functions, who controls it and the outcomes it delivers can be challenged through a societal sector of the economy and the political rights which flow from reform.

In a societal economy, profit as a measure of performance, like our natural being, and commonality which centres on the average, stretches across a broad spectrum. A societal appreciation of profit is related to the good it can achieve, and the public, not private, 'wealth' it can create. In contrast, the private sector occupies one extreme end of the profit spectrum, yet, it has overwhelming power to determine how our economy and society function, and the values we imbue as a society.

We live on this natural spectrum constrained by our bodies, brain size and lifespan. Having similar abilities, aptitudes and outlooks helps us live together in our society. Fluctuations too far from the average can cause distress and danger (with climate existentially so) but also provokes ingenuity and change. However, our economy elevates exceptionalism, rewarding people who possess skills and enjoy opportunities many of us do not, with ambitions for life many of us do not share. Our society progresses through individual ambition, and benefits accrue to exceptional individuals. But our economy can be designed to intrinsically promote the best outcomes for the majority too.

The societal economy is the missing link, which joins societal need and purpose with how our economy functions, instigating change where evolution has failed by creating a societal enterprise economy which co-exists and competes against the private sector. It challenges our current framework and assumptions.

Free markets are neither good nor bad, simply the rail tracks along which our economy travels, but the enterprises which currently serve them limit the good society can extract from them, and the share of national wealth which is collectively 'owned'. We can conceive a system which embraces market forces, fosters entrepreneurial spirit, and accepts the reality of markets and the profit motive, yet asserts collective rights over the economy. Market societism is that system, operating for societal benefit, a point where personal and collective self-interest converge. The paradigm leap market societism asks us to make, is that we see markets as the solution, not the inherent problem, to achieving fairer outcomes. Markets served by a societal sector function for our collective best interest. Markets only fail us because we cannot see beyond them being served, at scale, by companies operating for private sector interests. The failure is not in market economics but our diminished imagination to use them for reasons, and in ways, capitalism does not intend. We return to the question, if not capitalism, what?

The private sector seeks acknowledgement for its successes but where it fails, responsibility is pushed back to the state, and often the government pushes it back onto society. If unaddressed, the inequities that flow from inherent failings in our economic system are allowed to persist in our communities, dead weights that divide us, based often on discriminatory economic and social opportunities, and outcomes. Societal interventions for our personal and collective, common good, driven by shared values remain, as they always have, our last and often only resort in times of greatest need.

The Keynesian settlement empowered the State, not the general population. It allowed capitalism to assert monopoly rights, associated with property ownership, over the market economy, whilst leaving the general population to pick up the costs of systemic economic

The development of a societal economy draws on their foundational values and is one embodying their aspirations.

The triptych to which I refer above is completed when society is determined to be a unique and separately identifiable political and economic entity, attaching the general population to the market economy through a societal sector, supported by a political party which expressly commits itself to Society and its best interest, as part of its core philosophy.

This challenges the existing paradigm, in which producer ownership attaches shareholder interest to the economy through the private sector, supported by the Conservative party, which advocates a system based exclusively on a capitalist market economy.

The political stakes could not be higher. In a societal framework, the radicalised centre ground of politics stretches from what we identify currently as the radical left through to the liberal right. Conservatism, like its view of the market economy, lays towards the furthest extreme of the electoral landscape. It is no coincidence that a redefined societal political spectrum, has its economic counterpart; the greater part of the profit spectrum which is societal.

I have become increasingly aware how Plato spoke the truth when he observed how we adhere to fixed systems and resist change necessary to bring about greater equality. Why should this be so? In part because the fellowship of those who seek greater economic justice is fragmented. We plant our ideas, seeds into a soil that is not ideal, and will not nurture them into the economic and political landscape we visualise. We compromise our endeavours by failing to agree upon a ubiquitous system reflecting our values. It is too easy to accept that all ideas have been tried before, will not work, or exist through current forms and structures already, when this is not so. Our response should be to link our fellowship's values to an economic system unique to our aspirations which resonates politically and electorally.

Thomas Kuhn, the philosopher, writes of current paradigms, frameworks of assumptions, principles and methods which dominate. We try to deal with systemic anomalies but are bound by our current worldview and set of norms, and do not evolve gradually to the truth. We attempt to fit policy into the existing system, even though that framework prejudices its effectiveness. There is no clearer example of this than in the matter of the economy.

Max Planck went further, suggesting it requires a new generation to challenge the existing 'truth', and grow familiar with a new school of thought, as older generations die out. We should not live bound by the inheritance of older generations before placing younger, and future generations, and our responsibility to them, at the centre of our search for meaningful change.

The question of what makes an economy wealthy is only part of our search for a more just economy, for we must also ask, what economy makes our society healthy? Market Societism, a Societal Economy and the Politics of Society.

Chapter 1

Imagine – An Introduction

There are many Beatles games. The original one played in the early 1960s was, "who is your favourite Beatle?" my one, the question I pose is, "who is the most influential Beatle and in what way?"

The first guitar chord of a Hard Days Nights, a song title taken from an expression Ringo Starr used, strong, expectant, and ever so slightly discordant evokes a sense of energy and change, the nostalgic good vibrations of youth. You may be of a different generation, but I am sure the music of your youth can, like mine, power time travel too. That chord, George Harrison's "an F with a G on top" and instrumental licks, John Lennon's rasping, beseeching voice, and Paul McCartney's rhythmic bass and vocal, create momentum, in the moment we can all "feel alright". There was nothing complicated, just a group of friends making superb music how they did then, and would continue to do, in inexplicable ways, inspired, writing songs together, and generously gifting them to one another.

Beyond the achievement of their music the Beatles challenged conventions of deference, their influence one of irreverence. John spoke to political issues, often misinterpreted, informed by philosophy and existentialist concern he sought to improve the world demanding we should live in peace. In 1969 Yoko Ono and John held two weeklong protests against war, and attracted some support, but also widespread criticism, if not of their motive, of their action, with one headline describing them as "nutters" and another "hairy hedonists". In wider society I suspect, there was incomprehension of the values and forces driving Yoko and John to make their stand in the expressive, public way they did. However, in February 2003, three decades later, a social movement driven by the very same values Yoko and John were ridiculed for by many commentators in 1969, inspired between six and ten million people to vent their opposition to the Iraq war in protests and political events across six hundred cities. These protests did not stop the war, but it did show that the mainstream values a significant part of society held had progressed.[1] Perhaps John Lennon would approve Schopenhauer's observation, that truth passes through three stages, ridicule, violent opposition, and finally self-evident acceptance. It is whether our system of economy can be a just one that is one aspect of our search for truth.

George Harrison understood the importance of self, an awareness and understanding of personal belief and virtues. He identified as a spiritual person. Like John he searched for existentialist meaning, unlike John finding it in the beauty within, of a universal consciousness void of duality and ego. Whether one sees merit in George's philosophy is not the issue, what is important is the relevance of the self, of personal values. Economics is also about identity, personal and collective values, and how we are enabled by our economic system to live by them. The personal reflection on self, involving yoga, meditation, and mindfulness which George embraced are now part of many people's regular activity, when once, in Western everyday life fifty years ago these ideas and practices remained obscure. Society's values evolve, so should our economic ones.

The financial and public success the group shared failed to bring John and George the fulfilment they might have expected and led them to ask about materiality, self and values. These are questions related to our collective well-being too and how we organise our economy. There are societal issues concerning economic growth, wealth, values, well-being and happiness and our form of economy that we must resolve.

I return to the question: who is the most influential Beatle?

Think sausages. I would make a case for Linda and Paul, together with a little help from their friends at the Vegetarian Society. Informed by their appreciation of animal rights and conditions in slaughterhouses, Linda and Paul became vegetarians in 1971. In 1991, having first developed a range of vegetarian cookbook recipes, Linda and Paul launched Linda McCartney Foods. She also supported the protection of the rural environment and Friends of the Earth, engaging with social and environmental issues that today receive news coverage and are discussed across society daily, particularly on climate change and sustainable forms of economy. The food company she established was sold to Heinz in 1999, through their acquisition of United Biscuits who took over the brand in 1996. When it was first established some of the proceeds from the food business were to be used to fund her animal aid charity. This business was created by value driven objectives associated with animal welfare and driven by entrepreneurial ambition related to those values, social purpose, and profit. This driving force, and energy for profit and social purpose, exhibits one feature of an economy that can serve both individual interest and society.

The Beatles were fortunate, their success freeing them from personal, commonplace material and financial concerns, creating space for them to consider philosophical issues. This is a narrative of personal daily experience, we all have one, which determines how we relate to the world we inhabit. For many, if not most, as it would likely have been for the "Fab Four" had they not found success through their music, the day-to-day necessitude of living leaves little room for philosophical reflection. Yet, the search for economic justice relies on us stepping back and deciding first on the values and philosophy that informs our personal and societal relationship to the economy we wish to construct. Philosophy and values drove capitalism and statism, and we must agree what inspires our notion of economy for the collective, common good in this century and beyond.

At the time the Beatles disbanded, 1970, proceedings were initiated by Jane Roe asserting her absolute right to terminate her pregnancy without excessive government restriction. Like John Doe, the unknown, Jane Roe existed but not by that name, it was a fictional name to protect the plaintiff, Norma McCorvey; the same anonymity required to protect and provide a safe space for many women raising abuse issues connected to the MeToo movement fifty years later.

In 1973 the US Supreme Court decided in Roe v Wade that states could only draw statutes narrowly, to limit "fundamental rights", to protect their legitimate interests. In regulating pregnancy and abortion, the Supreme Court decided that states compelling interest was located at a point of "capability of meaningful life outside the mother's womb", or viability. Since 1973, there have been repeated challenges to this ruling. Fifty years later some US states have proposed heartbeat bills making abortion illegal as soon as a fetal heartbeat can be detected. In 2013 North Dakota passed such a bill, which was found by the Supreme Court to be unconstitutional following Roe v Wade. Recently, in this summer of 2021, Texas has introduced a 'heartbeat bill' banning almost all pregnancy terminations after six weeks gestation, standing accused of creating a bounty-hunting scheme because under the new rules legal action can be taken against anyone helping a woman to get an abortion, entitling them to $10,000 if they win. In 2020, the death of Ruth Bader Ginsburg led to a hasty rush in the dying days of the Trump presidency to ensure this liberal minded, consensus builder was replaced by a judge with less socially liberal views who might at some future date be part of a majority decision in the Supreme Court overturning Roe v Wade. It happened.

It is beyond the scope of this book to consider in detail the nature of society and change, and its relationship to rights, but there are some pertinent issues which emerge from this brief and selective social history.

The first is that personal values can change over time and meet little or no resistance. I can become a vegetarian, take up yoga, meditate or revise my opinion about what constitutes a necessary case for war. I may not see my values adopted by others, or government, but at least I am free to be the person I want to be, and hold whatever views I want, provided I do not break the law. However, societal change is more complicated. Deep held prejudice and ingrained behaviour, often associated with economic power, can be unchanging and immovable. The abusive behaviour of some men towards women, exemplified during the MeToo action, shows how slow we progress on some of the most important issues that determine quality of life based on respect and equality.

Second, in society we do not share a consensual view on many issues. Reasoned and unreasonable resistance to change arises as a constant; Roe v Wade is one such example. The competing views on the substance of life and the respective claims for protection, of potential mothers on the one hand and unborn children on the other, have not been resolved for over fifty years, and may not be for the next fifty years. This divergence of views is both legitimate and inevitable, and both views can be advocated through democratic institutions and process. It is a wonder of democracy that it enables such fiercely held contradictory views, even on the issue of the nature of life and existence itself, to co-exist within society. Society contains and is often animated by the diverse, irreconcilable views of individuals within it.

If democracy is to be fully representative, and we acknowledge we hold many competing, diverse and contradictory personal views, and values, then an economy should connect us to that diversity of values by exhibiting ubiquitous, distinct, plural features too, as should the philosophy and ideology that drives political process and policy. Too often, and to too great an extent, people do not experience outcomes which they are encouraged to expect. We need to restore the integrity between expectation and lived experience. An extension of the mixed economy to include more diverse corporate forms, and a focus on collective, societal, and shared values will help restore this democratic deficit, the disconnection between sections of the general population, the governed, and governments.

In democracies the electorate get to vote on these issues, but often without any sense of personal resolve on the issues that concern them; you can change the captain and crew on the ship as many times as you like, but if the ship is travelling in the wrong direction aggrieved passengers are going to mutiny. Governments can come and go, but if the economic system is not responsive and plural in nature then elections may have little effect in creating a unity of purpose across the whole nation.

Third, we are by nature individualistic, yet hold and share values attaching to our collective good. The terms of reference of our economic debate can be distorted by notions of individualism. It is an individual's right to be ambitious, to be entrepreneurial, to seek private gain, to become wealthy, however not all people share those aspirations. Many of us neither have the desire, ability, nor personality to make us successful by those measures. Our economic growth and economic outcomes are determined by the decisions of many individuals, remote from our concerns or well-being. In its exclusivity an economic system dominated by personal self-interest is unjustifiable. It leaves us thinking that equality and economic justice flows from opportunity, which it may for some, but we can see with our own eyes that opportunity for individuals considered exceptional rarely leads to systemic improvements in economic outcomes and improved well-being across our communities.

The Joseph Rowntree Foundation observed, having reviewed evidence from research on ethnicity and poverty, that there are definite patterns of disadvantage for people from minority ethnic backgrounds but that as soon as nearly every issue is examined in detail broad patterns start to break down.[2] One example given by them was of women from some South Asian backgrounds who wished to take care of the home and family rather than do paid work outside the home. This is a good example of a personal value and choice affecting economic outcome, one of many we make every day. We must answer the question, how do we build a just economic system that is inclusive, that increases the rights of women, in this example women choosing not to work in paid employment, to benefit directly from our joint economic endeavour; what are their economic rights and opportunities?

The issues surrounding poverty, opportunity, and ethnicity, however, go far beyond personal choice. In its 2019 annual report, the Social Metrics Commission observed that black and minority ethnic households in the UK are over twice as likely to live in poverty as their white counterparts. Approaching half of these households live in poverty compared with just one in five white families, evidence of discriminatory outcomes, but there is also generalised hardship affecting all in society.[3] The commission found that 14.3 million people were living in poverty including 4.6 million children. One cannot underestimate the tension which endures between the privatisation of profit, unequal opportunity, inequality of outcome and hardship, and the deleterious effect this has on social cohesion and well-being.

The poverty threshold or breadline is calculated by finding the total cost of the essential resources an average human adult consumes in one year, the largest expense typically being rent. As the founder of a societal organisation advocating innovative ways to create affordable societal market tenancies, it comes as no surprise to me that the dysfunctional, imperfect market for homes has impoverished lives. What is more surprising is that we fail to address issues adversely affecting vast sections of our population with sufficient application of purpose to find solutions through systemic reform, too often unprepared, seemingly disempowered, to challenge conventional policy that we can see with our own eyes is failing.

The Child Poverty Action Group report that one in five households in the UK have an income below the poverty line after housing costs, and 31% of children live in these households.[4] This level of child poverty is almost double the poverty rate of pensioners. The children and families affected by poverty are not minded to reflect on this data, for them it remains an issue of hunger, warmth, diet, health and quality of life. Well-being that more affluent sections of the population take for granted, is denied, and blights the lives of the poor daily.

The pervasive and enduring nature of inequality suggests existing policies based on redistribution through government borrowing, taxation and spending are not up to the job of reforming economic outcomes for too many of us. Our society is diminished by a fundamental misunderstanding of how our economy can work productively, and for our collective good, a prejudice that suggests wrongly, that individuality and endeavour for private gain is necessarily and exclusively the best model for enterprise, and that any alternative to the private sector must be based on state control, or not-for-profit and charitable social enterprise. There is a hybrid, ubiquitous form of enterprise and market economy which exists, one distinct and separate from private sector capitalism, that has the power to change outcomes in favour of our common good.

Imagine – In 1971, John and Yoko wrote the song Imagine. Ever the idealist, but a realist too, John asked us to consider a world with no heaven, no countries nor religion, "easy if you try". As for no possessions, he wondered if indeed we can imagine such a thing. We need some of John's social irreverence to challenge accepted norms of economic behaviour and presumption. It will remain a world of possessions but in redefining economic purpose away from an emphasis on individual want to collective need we can use our imagination and talents to construct a systemically more just economy based on policy, interventions and new forms of enterprise that are neither capitalist nor statist, a societal market economy.

Chapter 2

Inheritance – A History

I even think that the land of the entire country was hostile to marigolds that year. This soil is bad for certain kinds of flowers. Certain seeds it will not nurture, certain fruit it will not bear, and when the land kills of its own volition, we acquiesce and say the victim had no right to live.

Toni Morrison. 'Bluest Eye'[5]

We all have our own unique narrative which leads us to being who we are. Do our genes determine who we become, or our environment, nature versus nurture? As important, do we or should we care? Our economic system is an organic one, determined by our personal and collective history, and philosophy. It determines how our economy functions, our place, who we are within it, our lived experience, and the financial and social outcomes which flow from it. That economic history and philosophy is derived from two sources, our immediate experience and the outlook and world view we hold currently, but as important is the history and our collective reaction to it formed over many generations.

The British Academy, the UK's national academy for the humanities and social sciences, in its Future of the Corporation Project states explicitly, that, "Corporations were originally established with clear public purposes. It is only over the last half century that corporate purpose has come to be equated solely with profit".[6] In our search for a fairer, more responsible economy, there are two timeframes of relevance, first, the present, informed by recent history that shapes current attitudes. Second, we inhabit an economy driven by fundamental notions of enterprise and state that can be traced back over hundreds of years, particularly two hundred years from the furnaces in which modern capitalism was forged during the industrial revolution, and the politics of equity, derived largely through Marxist influence at that time. During this formative period, maximising profit was the principal aim of capitalist enterprise and to suggest otherwise misdirects our attention away from a historical narrative which helps us identify the nature of systemic reform required now and explains why we accept an economic system with so many intrinsic and inherent flaws.

Three hundred years before the Victorian industrial revolution, merchant adventurers set a template for enterprise that survives to this day. Lord Adebowale, Chair of Social Enterprise UK has said, "We created the limited liability company, and this was just as important as the invention of the steam engine".[7] The nature of joint venture through the joint stock company is of paramount significance. The limited liability company is a strand of DNA, that has carried the genes of capitalism into our existing economic body since the 16th century, even though modern society, largely influenced and designed in response to the political and social philosophy associated with it, would be unrecognisable to a Tudor, Elizabethan subject; a person subjugated to the Crown, with a submissive societal status. This status was determined in 1608, in Calvin's Case, to be the natural-born state of all those born within Crown dominions and is a term of definition used to this day.

To understand the values and forces that drive our modern economy, and disarm discussion about systemic reform, it is important to identify why the joint stock, shareholder owned company has become exclusively pre-eminent in delivering market based, for-profit economic outcomes. The question of what values informed the development of the limited liability company, its causation, takes us back even further in time.

In his Reith lecture in 2021 Mark Carney called for a moral compass to guide shareholders and entrepreneurs, part of an agenda for the reform of capitalism, by re-shaping the personal virtue of business owners rather than asserting collective rights to establish greater economic fairness. In the Q and A session that followed Mr Carney's lecture, Antony Gormley, the sculptor, asked a fundamental question, "is there another system"?, other than capitalism. This is the big question, the one this book seeks to answer.

The question I pose initially is, what makes the economy what it is? This question found its counterpart in an article Dr Naomi Fisher wrote on behavioural genetics and psychology, when considering how DNA makes us who we are.[8] Evaluating, what she describes as the compelling story of the evolving field of behavioural genetics in Professor Robert Plomin's book 'Blueprint: How DNA Makes Us Who We Are', she appraises his ideas on polygenic inheritance, that much of what we think is environmental is heritable, including that genes affect our environment because our behaviour affects our environment, making the environment heritable as well.[9] When speaking with Dr Fisher, the clinical psychologist Lucy Maddox stated, that regardless of what measure we use, what happens to us as individuals and the quality of our personal experience is important.[10] I asked at the start of this chapter whether we should care about who we are, about our economic being. Dr Fisher asks more succinctly, in the context of genetic and environmental inheritance," So What?". Her answer is that there are practical implications, that "the same environment is experienced differently by different people, and thus our attempts to change things through changing the environment will be affected by the genes of the individuals involved. This doesn't however, mean that we can't deliberately change the environment, and that the experience of the other person won't also change ...... our genes and environment interact in myriad ways". Our economy derives from similar dynamic interactions, a framework and beliefs rooted in our past, accepted behaviour and transactional daily experience that affect one another, and the economic environment and system we inherit. Our economic experience affects our economic environment and system in a behavioural and systemic loop. Our personal and collective experience of how the economy currently functions, limits our ability to conceive of systemic reform, rather, we rely on policies aimed at changing the existing economic framework, even though we know those policies will likely fail.

Economic DNA - Hierarchy, Private profit, the Limited liability company, and the Free Market

There is little doubt that in the English Civil War, my ancestor would have been given a pike, if not then some other agricultural implement, and ordered to line up alongside the Parliamentarians; it is my good fortune that he survived. I know this because as a child I was encouraged to attend our local Congregationalist church. Members believed each church should run its own affairs independently, and autonomously, with no need of outside authority. Further, I have little doubt that if an elder had ordered my ancestor to the front-line, he would have had little resource to oppose, but would have acquiesced. The effect of authority, hierarchy, upbringing, and a tradition of service and dues.

Two hundred and fifty years before this civil war, in 1407 the Company of Merchant Adventurers of London, a precursor of the modern limited liability company, was established by royal charter from King Henry IV, claiming liberties existing as early as 1216, just one hundred and fifty years after the Norman invasion of 1066, and the establishment of a regal feudal system. This Norman feudal system extended existing rights which kings and through them lords, enjoyed over property within their dominion, with all land being owned by the king and held by subjects on condition of service and obligation, homage, and allegiance, of vassal to king. The king sat on top of a pyramid, granting land to barons. Knights were granted land from barons, with the peasants, either villeins, bordars or cottars, and serfs, the poorest of the peasant class, and a form of slave, working manorial lands.

Feudalism impacts our culture today. We use words that can be traced back to Anglo-Norman French, through the Norman rulers use of language and dialect. These include asset, from the Anglo-French assetz and old French assez, meaning sufficiency or enough. Liability derives from the Anglo-French liable and French lier, to be bound by obligation. Our modern limited liability company, with the limited legal and financial exposure that shareholders enjoy, its language, derives directly from this meaning. Finally, justice comes from the old French word justice or jostise, from Latin justitia, meaning equity or uprightness. Shareholders equity references equality of rights between shareholders, a structural measure of equality absent in the language of the wider economy. Beyond language, we are hardwired to accept substantive forms of governance and structures of power whose roots are to be found in feudalism.

Adam Smith in the Wealth of Nations considered that the feudal system and its associated reliance on violence impeded development.[11] Marx considered feudalism to be defined by the power the ruling class achieved through controlling land, leading to a class-based society, reducing peasants to serfdom through labour, produce and money rents.

The legacy of feudalism impacts us today, an unseen hand, which through its foundational hierarchical principles, conditions us to accept an economic system where profit attaches to pre-existing wealth and status, with power derived from property ownership.

Unlike our feudal past, whose pervasive relevance appears lost in time, we continue to take collective pride in our ancient rooted common law right of equality before the law, presenting us with an attractive vision, that there is an enduring basal place where our common humanity determines how justly we are treated, beyond economy, wealth, and power.

Whether we are, or are not equal before the law, the idea that we are imbues our notion of economy too; we are encouraged to believe that we are equal as individuals in the opportunity privately owned enterprise offers for us to prosper. Margaret Thatcher put this argument concisely saying, with "capitalism and free enterprise there are no boundaries of class or creed or colour. Everyone can climb the ladder as high as their talents will take them". This reductive view of individual opportunity, talent, and aspiration, nevertheless articulates a conventional view that equality of opportunity exists for those who choose to seize it. Economic equality and justice become synonymous with opportunity not outcome. There is no right to equality within the economy commensurate to our right to equality before the law, yet both should have foundational status in an enlightened, democratic society.

The hierarchical structure of power which feudalism embedded in society, considered then and now as the inevitable and natural consequence of individual difference is significant. One hundred years after its establishment by royal charter in 1407, Henry VII granted the company of Merchant Adventurers a charter in 1505, whose members comprised trading investors, mostly mercers of the City of London.

The earliest joint stock company recognised in England was the Company of Merchant Adventurers to New Lands, formed by charter in 1553 with 250 shareholders. The self-interest of merchants was best secured through monopoly trading rights, and the Crown had the 'right' and power to grant them. Queen Elizabeth 1 granted the East India Company a monopoly on trade in the East Indies. By 1606 when the Virginia Company was founded, to colonise North America, individual shareholders were no longer responsible for actions undertaken by the company, and shareholders financial exposure, and therefore their personal responsibility, was limited, for they could only lose the amount of their initial investment. This model, then established, became, and remains the primary model for corporate ownership. These companies worked in essentially the same way as modern corporations. Collective corporate ownership reduced shareholders' personal and collective moral and financial responsibility for the actions of the companies they owned. This antecedence would be of no concern

but for the major effect it has had on defining our politics and economy to this day.

For the British crown to assert control over the slave trade to the colonies, in 1660 King Charles II granted a charter to the company of Royal Adventurers trading in Africa. This charter gave monopoly trading rights to his brother, James the Duke of York, later King James II. This was the natural path for enterprise; form a privately owned company financed by individuals to secure the profits from trading for themselves. Under the Navigation Act of the same year only English-owned ships could enter colonial ports. Monopoly, and militarisation, for private gain was effective. Ships sailed from Bristol, Liverpool and London to West Africa operating from military forts along five thousand miles of African coastline. Thousands of slaves arrived in the New World with the company's initials branded on their chests. There was no recognisable purpose other than to ruthlessly maximise profit, to colonise, and to control land and resource to generate future profits.

It can be observed that just as we continue to bear, collectively, the financial and human burdens of systemic economic failure, we currently share a moral responsibility for our nation's colonial past. Many people experience a natural, deep guilt for the suffering attributable to colonisation, yet it was only ever an inhumane venture instituted by the few, for the benefit of the few.

A hundred and twenty years after this company by royal charter had been established, in 1781, another syndicate, the Gregson slave trading syndicate sailed a ship, the Zong, with slaves on board. To increase the average price of their 'stock', one hundred and thirty enslaved Africans were thrown mercilessly overboard, into the sea to drown.

This narrative of colonial and racist history covers 120 years from the 1660 royal charter to the drowning of men, women, and children to maximise profit, and a further 250 years to our present day, when discriminatory, racially determined outcomes can be identified by the level of poverty in the BAME community relative to the general population. Its historic arc challenges the proposition that only recently has profit become the sole motivating feature of the joint stock company, it has always been so.

There are many positive achievements from commercial endeavour through the joint stock company, by shareholders seeking private gain: personal and social progress, economic growth, with trading surpluses generated, the tax on which has helped fund social and public expenditure. Through taxation and government's power to redistribute national wealth, a level of fairness ensures social cohesion is maintained. On the other hand, there are numerous examples of the failure of privately owned enterprise to deliver outcomes that are socially and morally acceptable, recently the financial crisis that was caused by unregulated debt instruments linked to speculative asset price bubbles, in 2008. The virtues or failures of private sector capitalism are well known, they are part of our daily discourse.

However, those judgements obscure the bigger issue, that the market economy should be plural, democratised and societised.

Feudal legacy, hierarchy and individualism are strands of our economic DNA, embodied in the limited liability, shareholder owned company, impacting everyone's lived experience. However, that alone would not necessarily have led to our over-reliance on monopoly capitalism. To do so required the oxygen of global, social, and political conflict, between capitalism and its nemesis, Marxian inspired communism, which condemned the planet to horrendous suffering during the cold war. This was a merciless battle for ownership rights over the economy, private or collective property rights, with a winner takes all outcome, that has squeezed all other meaningful options for the way our economy can operate from our consciousness. It was a binary, polarising conflict between two systems, both with foundational flaws, but justified by irrational certainty. The subjection of the individual, and collectively, societies across the planet, particularly during this period, is the epitome of power which corrupts.

In the Grundrisse, written during the winter of 1857-58, Marx describes the social alienation of people from aspects of their human nature, caused by living in a society of stratified social classes. That alienation from the self, Marx considered to be a consequence of being a mechanistic part of a social class, the condition of which estranges a person from their humanity. This is a view that many, if not most of us would share, from our own experience of self and the world, as we go about our daily lives, perceived not as a function of class, perhaps more likely of our identity, values, societal environment, employment, and income. He argued that society transformed from a feudal to capitalist society based on two social classes, defined by those who own and those who are employed. It is hardly surprising, having witnessed, with Engels, the effects of social deprivation and poverty associated with capitalism during the Victorian industrial revolution, of exploitation arising from control, a corollary of the ownership of capital and the employment of workers, that the Marxist solution would itself be reliant on a system of control and ownership, just not by capitalists.

The Victorian industrial revolution and this Marxist reaction to its unjust consequences created the seeds for the reality of what is our current bi-polar economy and politics. The proponents of industrial progress through capitalism and Conservatism adhered to the privately owned joint stock company. The Labour Party in the UK popularised and staked its electoral credibility on achieving equity through common ownership. Clause 4, adopted by the Labour Party in 1918, transplanted the aim of common ownership, its enduring socialist identity, into its lifeblood. Liberalism became marginalised at this point. Individual liberty became associated with free market economic liberalism, and collectivism with a 'socialist' aspiration embodied in the Labour party, that the individual would prosper most under the umbrella of the state. What remained undeveloped was an ideology asserting collective rights in the market economy, which embraced individualism but is neither capitalist nor socialist.

During this formative period, control and ownership was institutionalised through private sector corporate form, or state intervention and ownership, but what of society at this time?

It was only as recently as 1882 that the Married Womens Property Act, allowing married women to own and control property in their own right was passed, forty five years after Queen Victoria came to the throne; royal rule by a woman, according to accepted attitudes of hierarchy and authority did not translate into an appreciation of the rights of married women generally, or indeed your wife in particular if you happened to be a married man at this time. The Act which applied to England, Wales, and Ireland, but not Scotland, altered the common law of couverture. In English law the role of femme couvert was to subordinate her to her husband, putting her under the "protection of her husband, her baron or lord", a definition taken from Blackstone's 18th century Commentaries of the Laws of England, a literal and interpretative reference to the Norman legacy once more. Property passed automatically from wife to husband, and her separate legal identity ceased on marriage. Further, women were limited in what they could inherit, and the law of intestate primogeniture, which remained on the statute books until 1925, gave male heirs the right to all real property, land. This is just one, significant example of the patriarchal society which existed at this formative time. Inherited from ancient custom and laws, a system of control and ownership existed, exercised by men for the benefit of men over land, property, and person, giving men power, and disempowering women through their unequal legal and social status.

Given their lack of property rights and pervasive inequality, women's status as shareholders appears secondary. Nevertheless, it has been observed that individual women became more important in terms of the number of shareholders and the values of their holdings between 1870 and 1935.[12] The significance of 1870 was that until the Women's Property Act of 1870 a wife could not hold her own wages and investments independent from her husband.

The issue of women's equality is incrementally addressed, often through legislation giving specific targeted rights. The property rights given in the 1870 Act, and rights to equal pay fall into this category, as do established rights of property division in divorce. There is a more formal recognition of generic rights through legislation such as the Equality Act 2010, legislating anti-discrimination law, including gender discrimination affecting the individual. This construction of equality around rights attaching to the individual makes sense, given most people experience inequality and discrimination as a feature of their lived experience, part of their personal story. However, there is a collective, societal dimension to inequality, the extent to which women, but increasingly men too, support society through their role as partners, parents, and carers or as activists, rather than their economic contribution as employees or employers, making a positive contribution to our communities which restricts their mainstream economic opportunity. At no time in our history, particularly during the formative period, from the era of Victorian capitalism to the modern era, have we acquired a sense of societal contribution and concomitant reward that recognises this contribution.

My great grandparents were born variously between 1864 and 1874, only one generation beyond those I remember from childhood, around the time Marx wrote Das Kapital, by which time Britain had embraced free trade. The world that they were born into was harsh, as part of a labouring class employment was insecure. Sanitary, and housing standards were poor with many people living in overcrowded conditions. Henry Mayhew recorded these conditions, leading to "misery, ignorance and vice". Wider society often remained unenlightened, ignorant of the condition of the poor and the causes of poverty, compromised by prevailing notions of responsibility. It was widely assumed that improvidence and inherent vice were attributes of the poor; everyone had their place in a divinely ordered, and ordained, hierarchy. Observing these societal attitudes to the poor, Barbara Daniels cites Cecil Frances Alexander's 1848 hymn:[13]

The rich man in his castle
The poor man at his gate
God made them, high and lowly
And order'd their estate

Rights were subordinated in favour of patronage and philanthropy. Philanthropy was essential in mitigating the effects of poverty, with many of our modern charitable institutions emerging at this time.

During this period, when the roots of our bi-partisan economy and politics were planted, there was no meaningful electoral, parliamentary franchise. This is a compelling part of our historical narrative. We live with a similar political void today, with much the same consequence. Universal franchise is of recent origin, achieved within living memory. Indeed, we did not enjoy a fully representative franchise at the time of the birth of my father in 1919, a century ago, by which time our economic system was already established. The total registered electorate in 1880 was 3.04 million, less than one in ten of the population. It was not until the Representation of the People Act 1918 that the franchise was extended to men over the age of twenty-one years, whether they owned property, and to two fifths only of adult women. It took a further ten years for women to gain electoral equality. The 1918 Act also institutionalised the first-past-the-post system which also influences outcomes and restricts our ambition to reform today, by restricting access to parliamentary power, embedding the two-party ideological conflict of a bygone age.

One strikingly honest piece of legislation, affecting Northern Ireland, illustrates the connection and historic link between franchise, capitalism, and real-world power, just one of many unheeded warnings of 'troubles' to come, sixty years ago. The demand, one of five primary ones, made by the Northern Ireland Civil Rights Association, in 1967 was for "one man, one vote".

Until the Electoral Law Act 1968, which took effect in 1969, and the Electoral Law Act (Northern Ireland) 1969, owners of business were allowed to cast more than one vote in elections, including parliamentary ones. Owners of limited companies were allowed to cast more than one vote, and able to appoint nominees to vote across constituency boundaries. Part cause, part symptom, of wider social injustice which tore Northern Ireland apart, based on religious, societal, and economic difference, it indicates how the roots of undemocratic power can endure, until that is, they are challenged.

Our system of economy reflects the undemocratic nature of society at the time of its development. It still needs to be reformulated, in accordance with modern, democratic principles.

It has been observed through our virtual time travel, from 1066 to 1928, the foundational period during which our economic system developed, approaching a millennium, that there was little societal perspective, gender rights were limited, racial discrimination led to savage inhumanity, and the impoverishment and abuse of workers was endemic. Further, there was no universal franchise. A capitalist economic model, the politics which flowed from it, and the Marxist response to its inequities, was based on long established, and often ruthless patterns of hierarchy, patriarchy, control, and ownership, with rights attached to property. The privately owned, limited liability company, was the vehicle which transported these attributes, and values into the modern market economy. Whilst this economic system was unsuited to meet the needs of

Victorian society, philanthropy mitigated some of its worst effects. Conservatism became symbiotically attached to capitalism and the private sector, and Labour became, through Clause 4 of its constitution, committed to a socialist identity, real or increasingly over time imagined, based on production ownership. By any modern understanding of equity and societal rights, this system is fundamentally flawed.

A re-imagined history

After years of campaigning by the Suffragette movement, on 2nd July 1928, the Representation of the People (Equal Franchise) Act 1928 was passed. Women at last had electoral equality with men, giving the right to vote to all women over the age of twenty years, regardless of property ownership.

This marked a significant turning point in our economic and societal history. The influence of women in parliament helped place social values of support and collective welfare onto the main policy agenda. Reform to alleviate poverty and increase well-being was adopted through a multi-party system, where consensual policy making was valued, based on free enterprise through a vibrant privately owned sector, a societal sector securing the benefits of the enterprise economy for the general population, and with Government playing a supporting, interventionist role guided by a doctrine of societal best-interest.

The nation prospered. A plural society, with strong democracy and respected governance enjoyed an economy that was fair, with financial, gender and race equality its bedrock. Just as equality under the common law was an expectation all subjects shared and valued, so fairness for the common good became the collective aspiration of most citizens, allied to a system serving their personal and collective self-interest.

Of course, this alternative universe did not emerge during the 20th century, and we live with the consequences today. Perhaps our notion of enterprise and economy would have changed as society evolved but for the trauma of the cold war.

The cold war, lasting from 1947 to 1991, its 'iron curtain' separating nations and continents across the globe, was inevitable given the bipolar, competing claims of private and state-controlled capital, over land, peoples, and resources. That dividing world is encapsulated in the photograph of the "Big Three" at the Yalta conference in 1945, of Churchill, Roosevelt, and Stalin. Two competing philosophical tectonic plates collided, causing economic and political trauma from which we have not yet recovered; we live with its legacy.

Nation state fascism in the 20th century, built on national, economic self-sufficiency and state or productive capitalism, opposed international free-market capitalism, and international socialism. It was the antithesis of a society in which the rights of the individual were respected, subverting those rights in favour of extreme, dictatorial authoritarianism, to force society to mobilise for conflict, believing it would also lead to national unity and a stable and orderly society. It was the antithesis also of liberal democracy, attached to free market capitalism.

The cold war was more than an ideological battle of systems and ideas; it was powered by two competing military establishments in a battle, not for hearts and minds, but for land, people, and power. We have similar, more blurred, less absolute ideological differences today, a richness and diversity that differentiates societies across the globe, but nation states are not living on the constant brink of world war, though threats to peace emerge and remain. We have learnt to accommodate our differences, although the mentality of cold war division, the use of power to secure resources, strains relations. Nation states are economically interdependent, but ideologically independent of one another. Whilst espousing superiority in their systems of economy and governance, countries trade and function; they co-exist. The Cold War's polarising dichotomy was not false, but it was, and remains, paralysing. It led to a limited choice of government for the people of the UK, and no choice for the people who inhabited the lands of many countries across the globe.

During the cold war of the 20th Century, ideology became weaponised, the demarcation lines clear for all to see, and was used by governments to justify their military response. If governments positioned towards society and its common good first, what would drive a country to war, or militarism, other than imminent threat and preparedness to meet it? Too often the politics of power, control, and ownership drive conflict, not the politics of society's best interest. Cold war rhetoric resonates today, and we must beware of voices calling for a military response to opaque threats, often associated with economic power. This is the schema of past conflict.

Trauma and legacy

If an individual suffers trauma, or has developmental experiences in their life, their future self can be affected. Not only can the person be changed, but their understanding of who they are can be substituted. Behavioural patterns change throughout our development, based on life settings, social constructs, evolution of personal values and the expectation of others. We adapt our behaviour throughout life according to lived experiences. If this applies to an individual, could it not also be true for our collective self, affected by our shared experience. One may have anticipated that, from the 1920s to our modern era, with a widening electoral franchise, and a developing notion of individual rights within a more equal society, politicians and economists would have adapted the market economy to make it operate inherently more fairly, to achieve better social outcomes for the general population, but they have not made that foundational change. We were denied this progressive reformation by the catastrophic perfect storm I have referred to, a coming together of inherited patriarchal, hierarchical systems of ownership and control, finding their form in two opposing views of economy, and society, that became existentially opposed. The effect was to restrict, limit and reduce the economy we could conceive, based on false narratives and preconceived views that subsist to this day. We failed to healthily adapt.

As individuals we evolve, creating a narrative of identity based on experience, and healthy and unhealthy responses to those experiences. It is the same for our collective economic self. We need to redefine our societal and economic identity, and evolve, to adapt our economy to the changing realities and values which society, and the global community of people, if not nation states, share. It is relatively simple to change, a matter of diagnosis, changing one's behaviour, and self, with application. It is far more difficult to see beyond one's experiential self and identify the need for change in the first place, which requires the will to seek a new self. This is the task before us and the opportunity which societal economics gives us, to reshape our future economic and social being, and our future experience of life.

Once seen through new eyes, using a lens of societal best interest, perspective, and insight, we can reshape foundational aspects of our economy, challenging accepted orthodoxy, about the nature of the free-market, profit, public expenditure, investment, indeed the very purpose of the economic system itself. This reformulation has profound political implications related to economic rights, and the well-being of the general population.

Our inheritance, of ideas, frameworks, and social and economic ecosystems, particularly those derived from the Norman Conquest to the cold war, determine the nature of our economy and politics today. Through the limited liability, shareholder owned company, and its attachment to the free-market, we have exported a form of capitalism from the UK that is true to its adherent's values, one that has determined the bi-polar nature of our politics. There is however an alternative economy, one that can be built on collective principles, a societal one that embraces the freedom of the individual, but also operates for the common good; one that is neither capitalist, nor statist, but whose threads can be woven into the mixed economy. We come full circle, to the cold war, and beyond it, to the fall of the Berlin wall, by which time Linda and Paul were about to set up their for-profit, purpose driven vegetarian food production business. By this time our economic self was formed, an identity we need to understand, and whose attributes we need to challenge, to construct an economy that is inherently fairer, and that can help build a society more at ease with itself.

They say you can't grow
This land is too barren.
The dirt is too cracked.
This rain is too toxic.

..........unlike what you have been told
You are powerful beyond measure.
Your roots can persevere.

And you as a marigold will bloom
Unfolding your petals burning with beauty
Red and yellow
Orange and gold
Ready to boast to your colours

Alissa Jacques, Extract from
'They say you can't grow'[14]

Chapter 3

SOCIETISM and MARKET SOCIETISM

SOCIETISM: a social and political philosophy that promotes the well-being of the group, of society, without sacrificing the significance of the individual. Its economic counterpart, MARKET SOCIETISM is a system of economy in which enterprise operates for profit and societal purpose, through companies that are neither owned privately by shareholders, nor owned or controlled by the state. It is a system of trade, industry and government that promotes the common good and societal best interest, through forms of control, governance and intervention asserting collective and individual rights. Societal best interest is determined through the convergence of personal and collective self-interest.

Our natural social and economic being

"Are we all capitalists and driven by individualism? No. Are we all socialists or collectivists believing in the pre-eminence of the State? No. Are we all societal, individual beings, living collectively, together in society? Yes!"

This simple statement is self-evident. The paradox, the one that leads to economic injustice and social inequality, is that although we are all societal beings, our economy does not operate directly, inherently, and intrinsically for our collective, societal best interest. Society has yet to be determined a distinct, identifiably separate social, economic, and political entity.

We live in a market economy dominated by companies owned by private shareholders and are governed primarily by a Conservative Party promoting an exclusively capitalist, for-profit market economy. Opposition comes from those who promote state intervention. We do not enjoy an economy which reflects the breadth and depth of our society, nor many groups within it, who remain marginalised or disadvantaged. There is a universal cost too, for we all pay more for many goods and services, enjoy lesser benefits, and have fewer economic rights than we should, rights of choice.

Prevailing definitions of capitalism betray our current, diminished view of how an economy can function and its polarised form. It is variously defined as an 'economy controlled by private owners for profit, rather than by the state',[15] an economy that is a market economy rather than one which is centrally planned as a command economy. What is missing is any definition of a for-profit market economy, other than a capitalist one.

The politics of working status or class which flow from this economic settlement, of capital and labour, is outdated, part of an old-world order, but one which continues to dominate our modern age. The politics of self and class associated with individual identity has emerged forcefully, yet our political parties have failed to recognise this societal evolution in its fullness, and adapt their foundational purpose, leaving large swathes of the electorate disconnected and unrepresented.

Human nature, the part which values interdependence and common well-being, and on which our species has relied for its development, is compromised by an economic system based on individual exceptionalism and private gain. Consumerism has become over-identified with personal want, when it can also serve that want, and needs, but also interest beyond self, through virtue consumerism, supporting a societal sector.

In a moving quote given by Marcus Rashford for his campaign to mitigate the effects of child food poverty (let's#endchildfoodpovertytogether) he expressed his societal perspective, values and aims perfectly, evoking powerful imagery of a child needing food, rest, and security, safe in the knowledge that they are loved and cared for. Further, that we can achieve change collectively, together, saying:

"We must act with urgency to stabilise the households of our vulnerable children. No child in the UK should be going to bed hungry. Whatever your feeling, opinion, or judgement, food poverty is never the child's fault. Let's protect our young. Let's wrap arms around each other and stand together to say this is unacceptable, that we are united in protecting our children. Together we can end this problem."

This is bottom-up pressure demanding action, an assertion of collective values, instituted instinctively.

Societal values, collective ones we share, rooted in concern for others beyond self, flow from deep held, humane ethics. Values for the common good, demanding equality, fairness, and justice, need to be attached to the market economy if it is to inherently deliver well-being outcomes, increasing health and happiness. Our lived experience and our society are determined by the values which underpin it, and those values which are embedded through the economy. There can be no greater issue before us, than what type of society, and world, do we want to live in, and which values do we want to live by. This is a good starting point.

Values, Rights and Well-being

Values and the Common Good

The Common Good Foundation acknowledge that we live in a society in which the state and the market are both strong, even though both models have failed over the past half century. The foundation has a mission, to reconcile estranged interests and encourage mutual flourishing within a shared notion of the common good.[16]

The concept of common good developed through the work of many political theorists, moral philosophers and public economists refers to either what is shared and beneficial for all or most members of a given community, or what is achieved by belonging, participation and our collective action in the realm of politics and public service. Like well-being, the common good is a measure of outcome, not the description of a system delivering that outcome. A societal economy is designed to deliver well-being outcomes, underpinned by the notion of the common good.

The connection between values, and our determination of the common good makes it a definition unique to community. In practice it also depends on who is determining the common good; an authoritarian dictator will be unlikely to think the common good relates to personal choice and values associated with free will. One person's common good is another's perceived ill. We do however share universal values, usually related to humane ethics related to suffering and the basic qualities of life.

In economy, the common good is determined largely by the societal purposes leading to well-being, which attach to non-profit objectives, and the use of profit that would otherwise be distributable to shareholders but is not confined to this.

The difficulties defining what we mean by the common good can lead to obfuscation. Is it in the interests of the common good that our nuclear weapons armoury is increased, or rather that we seek a reduction in the number of warheads because society benefits, existentially in this case, from peace. Is greater nuclear defence, with its intrinsic offensive capability, a policy for the common good or not, or indeed is it a policy that ensures peace through the deterrence of mutual destruction, a policy of war that serves the peaceful outcome that society hopes will persist. Is it even a policy determined by societist principles, or statecraft and real politick rather than the politics of human values.

There is an inherent tension between state and society, government and the governed, just as there is between the economics of the private sector and societal need. This is inevitable, our democratic institutions, policies government and opposition parties advocate, and our election process regulate this tension. One virtue of democracy is that any elected party who governs in a way that offends the common good is unlikely to be re-elected.

The common good and public interest share similar characteristics, and it is reasonable to suggest that over definition of the common good would be counter-productive, instead like the idea of the public interest it is a guiding concept that emerges and evolves over time.

However, there are clear distinctions between the public interest and the common good which go to the heart of societism, its relevance and radicalism. Public interest is a core theory of democratic government, a statist benchmark providing a criterion for deciding policy that is essential, informative, and technocratic. It is a concept introduced into the existing framework and ideology of our body politic, a necessary one which acknowledges the constancy of wider claims and responsibilities that reach beyond sectarian interests. In contrast, the common good derives its meaning from the will of the people and their right for policy to be made for their benefit, rooted in ancient customs and rights that can be traced back centuries before the development of the modern economy. These rights have been subverted over generations, the rights of the commons; it is instructive that the people's parliament is known as the House of Commons because it represents a community of interest. If the House of Commons exists to represent community, it is appropriate that it includes parties ideologically and explicitly committed to the well-being, common good of community, of society.

We have a sense of and can usually discern what is or is not beneficial for ourselves and our fellow citizens, for the common good. This is largely because the essence of the common good is the same as the concept of equality before the law, it is a basic tenet of values, rights, and well-being.

We share a fundamental belief that we should all be equal before the law, of legal egalitarianism, that we are all subject to the same laws of legal justice, affecting our expectation and experience of equality, fairness, and justice. If we do not experience equality or justice, or systems persist that are incompatible with it, then our 'right' to equality before the law is offended, and collectively we often demand change. If those demands are not listened to, and policy changed, then the result is often a breakdown in social cohesion, disaffection and alienation leading to resentment or rebellion. We can trace this path of causation; it led to the abolition of slavery, the universal franchise, the riots in our cities in the 1980s, and most recently the Black Lives Matters and Metoo movements. These issues arise from incredibly complex forces, but share a common root, inequality that offends principles of universal justice and human rights, which in the UK is embodied in the convention that we should all be equal before the law. Unfortunately, convention does not always guarantee outcome, nor secure a right of redress.

The United Nations, rather than relying on convention, codified this fundamental right through Article 7 of the Universal Declaration of Human Rights which states: "All are equal before the law" and entitled to equal protection under it. Translated into over five hundred languages, drafted by representatives across the world from different legal and cultural backgrounds this right was proclaimed in 1948, identifying and asserting a universal, global value. Equality under the law is asserted regardless of race, gender, colour, ethnicity, religion, or disability.

The dome of the Central Criminal Court is crowned by a bronze statue of Lady Justice. She appears inviolable, unconquerable, and fearless, looking to a horizon above the heads of the public below. She personifies the moral judicial force, and fair judgment, that all those who enter the Old Bailey will, or should, expect to receive. She does not wear a blindfold because impartiality renders it redundant, justice is not blind. Beneath, etched into the stone above the entrance is inscribed the injunction "Defend the children of the poor", a recognition that power must be used to defend the vulnerable and that we should all be equal under the law and receive justice. These are the horizons to which Lady Justice looks, those of universal human right which should not be corrupted by power. This universal declaration of a child's right to justice is taken from Psalm 72. We must ask ourselves why it is that legal rights which underpin society, based on human rights of equality, protection and the responsible exercise of power are not applied in the matter of our economy. If children of the poor entered the Old Bailey to be confronted by a judge, predisposed to convict and a jury, unrepresentative of the public, who had decided on a child's guilt before the first word of a case was spoken, we would demand change. Are we then to defend the children of the poor today in our economy or abandon them? There is no fence to sit on here, it is a choice we should all make. There are far more children affected by financial inequality and poverty than legal injustice appearing before the courts. Do we conceive and implement a system which can eradicate child food poverty, leading to greater fairness across our economy or not, if not, why not? Societisation gives us the how.

The highest goal our political class can aspire to, one shared by the fellowship of those who seek reform of our economy, is to elevate the principle of equality, justice, and fairness within the economy, and accord it the same status we do our expectation of equality before the law. Rights and obligations flow from this foundational, societal principle that mandate a far-reaching reassessment of who our politics and economy work for, and the values we share as a society.

Equality, Fairness, and Justice

Governments determine the policy of state, influenced by and reflecting their philosophical values and beliefs. In the UK, the symbiosis of private sector capitalism and Conservatism, the dominance of Conservative government, and the failure of the Labour Party and the parties of the centre, particularly the Lib Dems, to revise their ideology and view of economy, to enable them to present a credible vision of an alternative economy based on societal values, has had disastrous consequences in the search for equality, fairness, and inclusivity.

Equality is commonly defined as the state of being equal, especially in status, rights, or opportunities. Social equality includes civil rights, freedom of speech, property rights, and access to goods and services within society. Capitalism prides itself on the merits of individual attainment, of individual exceptionalism, privatising wealth creation for the benefit of the few rather than the many; it is designed to produce inequality.

Inequality, often arising from discriminatory processes, leads to discriminatory economic outcomes that would be deemed unacceptable, compelling action in any sphere other than the financial and economic. Equality can be measured by statistics; however, its true measure is the impact it has on people's lives and in our communities. We all face difficulty in our lives, it is a constant. The Child Poverty Action group observe when asking the question, "who is at risk of poverty", life changes, such as unemployment, illness or family separation can happen to us all, leading to hard times when we find it difficult to make ends meet.

The group acknowledge that poverty is not something that happens just to others but is something that can happen to us all; increasing costs especially for essentials such as food, housing and fuel affect most people. I remember battling with British Gas over charges when my ninety-year-old mother, suffering dementia but still able to live at home, had been automatically placed on an expensive variable rate tariff. British Gas had systemised a default position that maximised profit despite a customer's age and vulnerability, an intrinsic feature of the motive of profit maximisation which drives capitalism. Prime Minister Johnson explicitly acknowledged and applauded private sector "greed" and "capitalism", when addressing his backbenchers in March 2021, crediting that motive of greed for the nation's coronavirus vaccine rollout in the UK. He later retracted the remark.

Life expectancy is currently 82.7 years for females and 78.7 years for men. However, there is a gap between the most and least deprived areas in England of 8.3 years for women and 10.3 years for men.[17] We can observe from these statistics that economic deprivation affects our most basic right, to life itself, a loss that if it were identifiable in hospital wards would lead to immediate action.

However, it also erodes healthy living. An even starker disparity was found to exist between those men and women enjoying good or very good health in the most deprived areas in England compared with the richest areas. Women in our most deprived areas enjoy 19.3 years, and men, 19 years, less healthy living than those in our most affluent areas.[18] A woman living in our most deprived areas might expect to live with good health for only two thirds of her life.

Economic injustice affects almost every aspect of our lived experience. It affects the impoverished person, results in a loss of human potential, and erodes the bonds that tie us together as a unified society. If issues of inequality are so profound and extensive then it is obvious to ask: why does economic inequality persist, and why have we been unable to address its causes comprehensively? A primary reason is that economic reform requires political engagement.

The Labour Party which once identified economic justice as its foundational cause linked to working class rights and working conditions, is failing to articulate a systemic alternative to market capitalism. It has failed to embrace into its core ideology, class rights related to identity, and general rights, in the same way it did working class rights, and to offer a credible vision of any system that can challenge Conservatism, particularly one grounded in the reality of market economics. To do this requires a reformulation of its socialist identity into one more electorally relevant to the modern age. The Labour Party has a rich socialist heritage, yet lacks the modern ideological framework linked to that heritage, which speaks to a modern society, confronting the reality of how the market operates against the best interest of those it seeks to represent. It is the "vision" thing.

The other parties of the Centre are values driven, or committed to the politics of nationalism, of national societal difference. The Liberal Democratic Party espouses liberty, equality, freedom, and well-being, of individuals and community. These values are in essence societal, yet they too fail to articulate an alternative vision of an economy that uniquely speaks to those values and addresses the intrinsic inequality that derives from market capitalism. They, like the Labour Party, are defined by their response to Conservatism and capitalism, not enlivened by any idea of an alternative, ubiquitous system which delivers more just economic outcomes. They are both driven by societism, concerned with societal best interest, but do not have the philosophical language to express it.

The Labour Party, despite increasing calls within its ranks for electoral reform, remains committed to the first past the post electoral system. The privilege this system bestows on the Labour Party has allowed them to indulge in internal debates over identity and ideology, secure in the knowledge that they will remain the main party of opposition in Westminster. The reality is that since 1979, other than during the Blair and Brown governments, Labour has not held power. The economic and social data of recent years has been dismal reading, and Keir Starmer should be, but is not, guaranteed to lead his party to victory at the next General Election. The Lib Dems, appear to believe that with one more push, the electorate will turn away from Conservatism in favour of their 'kinder' values and identity. Yet, the Party, with its antecedence in the Liberal Party, has not held power as a majority in government for over a hundred years. For two parties with such proud, rich, and relevant histories, to be left electorally marooned in this way has devastating consequences for the electorate they claim to represent. Arguably the same forces which render us collectively unable to conceive of systemic economic reform, affect these parties' abilities to evolve foundationally too.

In the film the Usual Suspects, Kint, a seemingly dishevelled and submissive character, possibly implicated in a crime of robbery and murder, presents a mythical, ruthless gangster, Kaiser Soze, as both mastermind and killer. Borrowing a line from Charles Baudelaire, he tells the detectives questioning him that "the greatest trick the Devil ever pulled was convincing the world he didn't exist".[19] This is of nothing compared with the myth we accept as self-evident truth in the matter of economy, which goes to the heart of endemic inequality. The fiction I allude to, is that "the greatest trick that capitalism has pulled is to convince the world that it and it alone maximises the creation of wealth and economic progress, and it and it alone reflects our innate human nature".

This fiction is sustained by the greatest paradox, that Marxist inspired socialism far from challenging capitalism has ennobled it, elevating capitalism to be our exclusive and predominant system of economy. This is reality, lived as tragedy for too many people. The command-and-control economics of Marxism and socialism, once of their time, is incompatible with free-market economics, addressing economy, as capitalism does, through its lens of control and ownership. Our failure to see beyond the political chasm of capitalism, or a socialist inspired alternative, needs to be corrected in favour of the market economics of societism.

We have been conditioned to accept a false dichotomy, that we have a limited choice between capitalism and non-market economics. This is not true. The choice is between a market-based system, capitalism, which operates for the benefit of private individuals, or a market-based system which operates directly for the benefit of the individual and collectively, society, which we can call societism.

Inequality is not only hardwired into the economic system, but it is perpetuated through a lack of equal opportunity, with the dynamic of unequal opportunity and outcome passed from generation to generation. Discriminatory features of our economy are evident in health provision and outcomes, education, employment, housing, and family and community welfare. It suits us to accept a false narrative around equality of opportunity because it assuages our responsibility to deal with inequality of outcome. It is a disingenuous position to adopt. It is based on the idea that we can control our own destiny through our individual endeavour, and all that stands before us and a life of comparative riches is our own ability and desire to work hard, a proposition advocated by proponents of the human virtues attached to capitalism which is incomplete and diminishes us. Once one accepts there is no meaningful equality of opportunity, then no longer can we hide from the plight of the relatively impoverished, or those disconnected from mainstream economic opportunity.

The idea that anyone can 'climb the ladder of success' and that there is equality of opportunity to do so is unrealistic. We inhabit a spectrum where most of us are by inescapable definition, average, and relatively few occupy the extremes of that range which are identifiable with individual exceptionalism, in any walk of life. This is a societal, national, and global law of nature and human being. However, reliance on personal exceptionalism resonates so forcefully that we adhere to the belief that an individual can be responsible for their life's fortunes, that by raising the level of individual attainment of opportunity for a few gifted individuals we are addressing an agenda of equality. This view of individual opportunity misses the point, that greater equality should be an inherent attribute associated with our economic system attaching to group well-being, as well as to individuals accessible through their exceptional endeavour and ability. The market economy should recognise our commonality and natural, average state rather than, or at least as much, as it does the exceptional extreme of our human being. Capitalism is justified, but monopoly capitalism is indefensible.

In September 2021 it was reported that KPMG, a leading accountancy firm, has set a target for the number of working-class staff, defined as those having parents with "routine and manual" jobs, differentiating the routine work of plumbers, butchers, van drivers and electricians from that of routine numerical calculation and interpretation.[20] It is commendable positive discrimination, which recognises that working and social class status, and the "invisible barriers" that exist for people from lower socio-economic backgrounds, affects opportunity and progression.

Revealingly, the firm had the courage to publicly acknowledge that less than a quarter, and only one fifth, of its partners and directors respectively were from working-class backgrounds. Its target is that 29% of partners and directors, little more than a quarter, should come from working-class parentage. It is noteworthy that this initiative, increasing opportunity for an exceptional few, acknowledges that inequality remains intergenerational, socially, and environmentally heritable, a disadvantage identifiable by parental social status, and that the professions are dominated by those from relatively privileged backgrounds. This is the economics of legacy and self, that you are defined by your inherited status.

The Social Mobility Commission estimate that, in Britain, people from a privileged background are 60% more likely to be in a professional job than those from a working-class background.[21] Bina Mehta, Chairwoman of KPMG acknowledged the contribution diversity can make to business performance and is reported as saying "Diversity brings fresh thinking and different perspectives". It is this diversity and the contribution which can be harnessed from it which systemic societal reform seeks, through diversity of corporate form and motivating values in our economy. The societal issue we face is not just about the opportunity of children from working-class backgrounds to succeed and raise themselves from working-class to professional status over their lifetimes, but rather, what of their parents and those who may be unable to elevate themselves? An economy should function to maximise financial benefit universally.

Inequality is bound to arise when financial rewards are accorded to exceptional individuals, when we are exceptional in other ways that are not linked to financial reward. The abilities that make a person successful in business may well make them very average were they to work in the caring services, or as a homemaker. Capitalism has twisted our sense of virtue in favour of its values and by extension, carried that view of success into society, particularly through the education system and goals for academic attainment. If you succeed as a homemaker, community or hospital worker, or carer, you may be applauded, but rarely are you described as being a "successful" person, an accolade usually reserved for those achieving financial success. A societal economy builds a more just economy, based on an expansive idea of rights and success, contribution to society and rewards.

The Women's Equality Party strive for greater and equal representation of women in positions of power, in politics, business and industry. They address sexual inequality at home through a campaign for equal parenting, caregiving, and shared responsibilities, and an end to violence against women. These aims identify group inequality with individual experience, and primarily seek progress through gender balance and respect. They find expression too through demands for increasing numbers of women to be promoted to the top of our hierarchical institutions and corporations, to break through the barrier of the "glass ceiling". From a societal perspective this is only one side of a coin, on the other is the issue of equality for those who, for whatever reason, may never wish to hammer on the glass ceiling, or may be unable nor have the opportunity to do so. The broad base of our population is excluded from direct access to the benefits our economy can provide them. Society suffers an economic and political vacuum, a void where the air of collectivism has been squeezed out of our body politic. The politics of society are the politics of equality from bottom to top.

Well-Being, Health, and Happiness

When I first read Richard Layard's groundbreaking analysis on the economics of happiness, and in particular his observation that happiness is not derived from absolute but relative prosperity, it struck a chord, the simplicity of an idea that once known seems obvious, the economic equivalent of motorway cats' eyes.[22] If social, political, and economic societism has any single defining purpose it is to address our well-being.

Professor Layard cites three factors that economists fail to take into sufficient consideration, if at all. It is not just economists who fail in this regard, however, but our economic system which is not designed for the purpose of fostering well-being, quite the contrary.

The first feature Professor Layard cited is relativity, that happiness is derived from relative as well as absolute income, and that relative aspiration can lead life to be experienced as a competitive, individualistic rat race. Second, he observed that the more one gets used to a higher income, the greater one's idea of sufficiency of income becomes, leading people to work harder even though this may not lead to greater happiness through a healthy work-life balance. Third, he stated that individual preferences are not constant but change according to trends and cultural norms. He concluded that a purpose of taxation, in addition to paying for public services and redistributing income should be to counteract the cognitive bias that causes people to work more than is good for their happiness. This is an issue of values. An individual has the right to determine what makes them happy partly through their own work-life balance. Some may choose to work hard, others to work less, developing and enjoying other aspects of their lives.

The cognitive bias that we share as individuals, which Professor Layard identifies as a deviation from rationality, based on a perception, a subjective reality of what makes us happy has its systemic, collective counterpart; our adherence and belief in a system of economy that we are conditioned to believe will make us happier, when in many ways it cannot. Again, this is an issue of the primacy of human values, of an economy reflecting self, or one of self within society, of personal reliance, or mutual self-determination and interdependence.

Lord Layard working in partnership with the Dalai Lama popularised issues of well-being and happiness through the movement, Action for Happiness, "of people committed to building a happier and more caring society….. to see a fundamentally different way of life – where people care less about what they can get just for themselves and more about the happiness of others".[23] The NHS offers five pointers to improving well-being: connection with people, being physically active, learning new skills, giving to others and mindfulness, paying attention to the present moment. Action for Happiness extends this list of factors and refines them, emphasising doing things for others, having goals, looking for what is good, being comfortable with who you are, and being part of something bigger, among its ten keys for happier living.

The increasing awareness and actions for well-being articulate what has long been known, as Robert Kennedy said in 1968, that prevailing measures of economic success, "…. measure(s) everything in short, except that which makes life worthwhile".[24] This understanding, reinforced by science and research into what increases well-being and happiness, together with global issues of sustainability and environmental responsibility, have caused populations worldwide to question the desirability of unrestrained capitalism, of wealth creation, and economic growth at any cost. Our economy, based on the exclusive primacy of capitalism imposes values on us that do not accord with those most associated with our collective and personal well-being, and those of our planet. The essence of our quest must be to reshape our economy so that it inherently reflects and responds to values of well-being beyond financial wealth. An economy that is both capitalist and societist would be one that derives the benefits of both systems.

By unifying society around shared goals, a societal sector addresses directly, personal factors affecting well-being and happiness, including shared purpose, contribution beyond self, introducing the idea of consumer as giver as well as purchaser, of interacting with meaning and purpose, as part of something bigger than ourselves, and participating in something that is good. Our consumerism can be beneficial beyond satisfying our personal want and need. What is good for us as individuals becomes good for society, challenging the notion that the market economy need necessarily be a place governed by selfish, or purely self-centred motives, challenging the lazy assertion that capitalism embodies our human nature.

A little personal anecdote: I was nine years old, three days to go until my tenth birthday. On Good Friday, 12th April 1968, the sun shone, and 36,589 fans turned up to watch West Ham play Nottingham Forest, the first of three games to be played over the Easter period. The day, the 6d programme, the team are a fond memory, my first game, taken by my dad, I was growing up. The team included Bobby Moore, celebrating his birthday too, Peters, Brooking, Redknapp, and Lampard, Ferguson in goal, big Billy Bonds in midfield, John Sissons on the wing, Stephenson and Dear. No Hurst, but I can still picture him in my mind's eye. No room to move, packed into the South stand, adults making sure children had a good vantage point, the players glowing, a different flesh pink, healthy skin colour I had never seen before. Why West Ham? I did not know, but there was an affinity between club and me, an identification of heritage, community and belonging. The Hammers were in a relegation battle, so often to be the case over the years, as our anthem reminds us poignantly, each new day full of dreams, bubbles flying high, nearly touching the sky, only, like the dreams, to fade and die.

As I write, the self-styled 'top' six clubs in UK football, four of which are not at the top currently, have agreed to be founder members of a break away European league from which they cannot be relegated, making their business model predictable and as one club director puts it, to maximise profit and revenue. West Ham indeed, like their bubbles, have floated to the upper echelons of the league this year and if the current positions in the league table remain at the end of the season they would gain, by merit, a place in the aptly named, currently constituted Champions league next year. The breakaway league challenges the pyramid structure of the football league system, attacking the soul and spirit of the game and its essence of competition, of success and failure. The reaction across the world of football has been visceral, a recognition that commercial self-interest takes no account of a football history dating back over a hundred and fifty years and that football tribalism is part of community, and beyond club loyalty, fans share a love of the "beautiful game". It may well be that the fans united will never be defeated, that consumer power will trump capitalism, but we shall see. The reaction from fans gives a glimpse of the extraordinary force that the power of societal politics can unleash, particularly when the private sector offends us. As the Leeds striker Patrick Bamford said, it's "a shame" that the reaction to the European Super League is not mirrored in the fight against racism and "all the things that go wrong". This is an appeal to the solidarity we have as members of our communities, of society, to solve problems by asserting our collective will.

The Prime Minister, one who praised and attributed the covid vaccine rollout to greed and capitalism, suggests an enterprise model should exist in which the fans have most voting rights. This is an explicit acknowledgement that there are indeed superior forms of enterprise that can serve our collective interests better.

The action taken by the owners of the 'top six' on the other hand is a perfect illustration of how private sector corporatism operates, with perfectly authentic and honest self-declared interest, to maximise profit irrespective of the well-being of community and the individuals who make it up. It is my perfect reason for being a societist.

An epilogue: The European Super League collapsed within three days, with all six English clubs announcing that they were pulling out, following an extraordinary backlash from fans, players, managers, and politicians.

Ubiquitous fellowship – internationalism and global welfare

I can only surmise how a person from another culture, living in a country far from me, under a system of government different from that of the UK, with its own, unique history, philosophical outlook, conventions, and familiarities, might relate to the values and outlook of their society. There is, however, increasing appreciation across our planet that we share values, universal aspirations and hopes. Societisation speaks to those largely instinctive beliefs, ethics and desires which often find voice in the call for a "better future", for humane, civilised progress, sustainability, and environmental awareness; a recognition of something beyond self, of planet and a global society.

An economy designed to serve the collective needs of society, as well as reward individual endeavour is a bottom-up, not a top-down system reliant on the trickledown effect of wealth and redistribution. The politics of society is of the people, bound by purpose for the common good to them, and as such challenges policy that offends universal human values and those of society. It is a philosophy which is of substance over form, not based on power, but one demanding representation. It can be contrasted with the ideology of sectarian interests and power which dominates global politics irrespective of whether governance is democratic, oligarchical, or authoritarian. The politics of society and the common good transcend traditional political boundaries, and is powerful which is why governments, regardless of ideology, often invoke the injunction that they "serve their people".

Once social and economic rights become identified with collective, societal outcomes, the ties that bind us globally and nationally will become more important than the politics that divides us. This is the politics of the environment, sustainable economics, human values and most recently covid.

The Davos manifesto 2020: the Universal Purpose of a Company in the Fourth Industrial Revolution, seeks the formulation of a "better kind of capitalism" by proposing that companies should engage all stakeholders in shared and sustained value creation, including employees, customers, local communities, and society at large. They state that the best way to understand and harmonise stakeholder's divergent interests is through policies and decisions that strengthen the long-term prosperity of a company.[25]

The motives behind this manifesto and the words are well spoken, but they continue to expound the false narrative around the shareholder owned company, the major stakeholders in capitalism, who are omitted from the Davos headline list. We should not settle, nor rely on a "better kind of capitalism" but rather devise a non-capitalist alternative that is altogether kinder.

The main purpose of the corporate shareholder is to make profit, more often than not, to maximise it. They may have other social purposes appended to their central aim, but one only has to look at the nature of corporate activity, and investment measures used in determining corporate valuations, to realise these companies are profit maximising, non-societal ventures. The fact that at the highest levels, governments, and the world leadership that Davos brings together are considering purpose beyond maximising profit, and acknowledge responsibility to community and society, is welcome and recognises that capitalism's failures cannot remain unaddressed. If they do capitalism could face an existential crisis, not just 'run of the mill' crises. The reference in the Davos manifesto to society confirms the validity of the proposition that society has a right to make collective claims on our economy.

It mandates not just a revision of capitalism for good purpose, but the institution of a societist programme, and entities that can reshape that economy on behalf of our collective, societal good. It is a recognition that capitalism is fit for a purpose, but not for purpose that leads intrinsically to our collective, common good; that comes through the societisation of our economy.

In September 2015, the General Assembly of the United Nations adopted the 2030 Agenda for Sustainable Development which included seventeen goals, building on the principle of "leaving no one behind".[26] The goals are worth restating and include: No Poverty, Zero Hunger, Good Health and Well-being, Quality Education, Gender Equality, Clean Water and Sanitation, Affordable and Clean Energy, Decent Work and Economic Growth, Reduced Inequality, Responsible Consumption and Production, Peace and Partnership, Climate Action, Sustainable Communities, Life on Land and below Water, and Industry, Innovation, and Infrastructure. These goals are identified as ones capable of "transforming our world". The UN helpfully specifies goals that through a revised "moral compass", governments and capitalism is encouraged to deliver. However, there is a constant tension between the basic assumptions underpinning a capitalist economy and the transformative goals that the UN refers us to. These transformative goals are societal rights, their delivery can be enabled through a system that can deliver outcomes that capitalism is not naturally equipped to even consider.

Climate change poses an existential threat to humankind. Every person and animal on our planet may have to adapt to survive, with inadequate action survival itself may not be secured. The evidence is clear, "the climate on Earth has been changing since it formed 4.5 billion years ago. However, since the Industrial revolution from the 1800s, the global temperature has increased at a much faster rate. By burning fossil fuels and changing how we use the land, human activity has quickly become the leading cause of changes to our climate".[27] There is a link between economy and climate change, responsibility, and our responsiveness to its devastating consequences. The correlation between rising temperatures and economic activity since the Victorian industrial revolution is clear, the product of an economic system that was and remains disconnected from societal best interest. In the most dramatic manner, the benefits of industrialisation have been reaped by the developed economies, and shareholders within those economies, whilst the costs and consequences have been passed from the private sector onto the global community, with every person having to bear the financial burden and non-financial, human risks of temperature increase. This causation, if no other, is so profound that a societal economic framework, and systemic reform becomes of global, ubiquitous significance.

The fellowship that seeks greater economic justice is wide, broad, and deep, indeed breathtakingly so. In every facet of our lives, every feature of our economy that manifests itself in an injustice or wrong, in which there is individual, group or systemic suffering or disadvantage, whether social or economic, human, or financial, there is a person or group of people who will campaign for change, motivated by a desire for good through better outcomes. However, in our diversity that fellowship becomes weakened, fractured, each calling for reform, like lonely voices shouting in the wind of a howling gale, often unable to be heard. That fellowship must unite under the umbrella of a system, philosophical, political, and economic, into which their individual programmes for justice can be woven. We need an ideology that can bear our collective weight, informing capitalism but offering an alternative path from it, that can be part of the Davos debates but be identifiably separate from it, giving voice to an alternative vision of economy. Societisation and societism offers that unique, ubiquitous, and separately identifiable system which our fellowship can mould, develop, and attach to, giving expression to our values.

The fellowship to which I refer is a global one, attempting to improve the lives of people across the planet. The UK can be a beacon of hope, promoting democracy attached to a societal, well-being purposed economy. Capitalism has disenfranchised and disempowered too many across the globe, through conquest, inequality, and acquisition for its adherents, the UK chief amongst them, to be heard as speakers with absolute integrity on matters of general well-being and societal good, no matter how much the World economic Forum, UN and national governments may suggest otherwise.

Finally, what of the people, citizens of our planet, the only form of life in the Universe that we know of, which has evolved to conscious, sensate maturity with the physical attributes, arms, legs, and minds, enabling us to determine our own destiny and quality of life.

The strength of our collective power, if not denied us by design or neglect including through technology and AI, can alter the way we behave and experience life for the better. It is nothing less than a battle for humanity between 'good' and 'not so good' virtues, ones sometimes turning to evil. If our government, and the fellowship who seek reform, and greater justice, claim to act in the common interest who do they act for if not the 'people', society.

There is a choice between universal values arising from distinct ideas of what our human nature dictates, a creed of thought built on the universal value of self and personal gain, or universal values associated with the commonalities of our existence. Perhaps for the first time, we have the power, knowledge, and ability to advocate reform without the need for physical conflict. Our guiding light should be that in whatever way we promote our collective, common good, however radical its implications, we should never sacrifice the significance of the individual and their right to personal, health, happiness, and well-being; it defines who we are as individuals, our society, and cause.

Well-being outcomes in a Societal Sector

Marcus Rashford's campaign, and the petition he organised calling on parliament to extend food poverty assistance into the 2020 winter, was motivated by his personal experience; as a child he suffered hunger, his friend's parents inviting him to eat in their homes to ensure he was fed and did not go hungry. His reaction to injustice he describes, as addressing an issue of "humanity" and that he would use his voice for those children who do not have one. His campaign group reported that 2.3 million children experienced food insecurity between August 2020 and January 2021. As many as a fifth of children live in households in the UK regularly beset by hunger[28], with 30% of children, and over a fifth of people, living in poverty. This level of human hardship, in the sixth richest country in the world by GDP, indicates a systemic defect in the way markets are served. In an economy of such wealth, achieving £205 billion of grocery sales per annum, generating profit, food poverty should not exist as a biproduct of how it functions.

Marcus Rashford formed The Child Food Poverty Task Force, a coalition of charities and food businesses calling on government to implement recommendations from the National Food Strategy. A full house, ten out of ten of the UK's largest food retailers, stepped forward to support the Task Force's initiative, a worthwhile commitment by them to mitigate the worst effects of child hunger in the UK. However, the systemic roots of child poverty, the intrinsic consequence of a supply chain maximising those companies' shareholder profits remains unchallenged. The National Food Strategy, an independent governmental review, was led by Henry Dimbleby, an entrepreneur, founder of Leon, the restaurant chain, a business strategist, and co-author on work to improve school food and education on food. The Strategy lists fourteen recommendations under four categories, four of which fall under the aspiration to "reduce diet-related inequality", making the link one between diet and inequality, not hunger and poverty. The passion Marcus feels, and his response to act, highlights to good effect the power of societal indignation, when an individual, animated by injustice inspires business and government to work together. However, it obscures the fundamental issue; how can an economic system creating such value, managed by people of considerable ability, serving customer's every desire, fail to be one which provides food for all at affordable prices? It is a system which gives great riches on one side of its scale but fails to alleviate hardship for many on the other. The economic cake is served up in unfair proportions, and for some their portion is too small.

As Marcus Rashford points out, those on the wrong side of that scale often have no voice. Disempowerment and hardship are causally linked, a foundational feature of our economy.

If we knew child food poverty could be eradicated or its effects mitigated in a simple and practical way through societising the economy, why would reform be denied us, why would any politician not wish to embrace such change. It is a good place to start.

Food Poverty – the role of the for-profit company operating for a societal purpose

You have a choice of two shops from which to buy your weekly groceries. These two shops are identical, they offer the same items, at the same cost, in the same shopping environment. One is owned by shareholders, and the profit the shop generates but no longer requires in the business is returned to them. The other is a societal company, after financing its core for-profit activities it uses its profit to establish express food stores in our twenty most deprived areas selling a basket of products at low prices, and supporting, by using the power of its supply chain, food banks in the charitable, voluntary sector. Which shop would you choose to buy your groceries from, and how would you feel, as a consumer purchasing from a shop with a social purpose? The private sector one operating to reward shareholders, or the one with societal objectives, in this case to mitigate the effects of food poverty by earning profit in open, market competition, and using it to for a societal purpose?

I have posed this question to many people, and all would choose to purchase from the company with societal purpose, suggesting consumerism attaches to social purpose in a powerful way. Virtue-consumerism in a societal sector can enhance personal well-being, beyond the satisfaction of wants.

The rewards, incentives, and pay for managing or working in a societally purposed business could be identical to those in the private sector. However, for many, the well-being associated with activity beyond self, and through connection to others, could be improved by employment in a company operating for shared, social purpose.

One cannot blame anyone for food poverty, it would be easier for us if we could hold someone accountable.

Food poverty arises because of inherent, intrinsic failings embedded in our economic system. In the 19th century, philanthropy was one of the few ways to mitigate the worst effects of capitalism and has been praised for its achievements. In 2020, the cause of alleviating food poverty show it remains so. Modern philanthropy, inspired by Marcus Rashford, and of those setting up and operating food banks, remains necessary to alleviate hardship. Private sector capitalism is remote from societal need, whereas a societal sector founded on societism exists to meet that need.

In food supply, private sector profit maximisation, and corporate shareholder purpose, makes capitalism ill-suited to the task of providing affordable food for all. There is sufficiency of supply, just not at prices affordable for all. In housing, we suffer the same consequence, unaffordability, and embedded inequality, to the detriment of those without pre-existing capital, particularly younger generations.

In housing, society does not suffer because of the dynamics of a privatised free market, sectoral monopoly, but rather the consequences of an imperfect market. The affordability of housing is an intergenerational issue. Consumers, particularly younger ones, pay inflated rents and prices for homes, because of insufficient supply, which fuels higher prices supported by conditions attached to the availability of credit, and planning controls restricting the availability of land. A major aim of a societal sector is to correct anti-competitive, market imperfections where possible.

The Housing crisis – solutions from a societal perspective

The housing market is broken and dysfunctional, housing policy is largely unfit for purpose. From a societal perspective, the policy of increasing the supply of homes by building more houses and flats is, in its exclusivity, a case of the wrong measure, targets, driving the wrong policy. Politicians can claim easy credit for plans to increase the rate of new build, and opposition parties can highlight inevitable failures as targets are not met. Shelter, the housing charity, estimated that three million new social homes are needed over twenty years, when only 6,500 were delivered in 2017/18.[29] Of all the homes developed on green field, Green Belt sites since 2015/16 only 10% have been deemed affordable by the National Planning Policy Framework definition of affordability.[30] The ever-spiralling price of houses and flats, deprives younger people from purchasing a new home. Many people wishing to start a family cannot afford to buy a property.

Supported by government loan guarantee schemes, and funded by mortgages at low interest rates, housing demand has exceeded supply leading to higher prices. Ever rising prices are the motivating force which drives a speculative element in the UK housing market. Cheap credit fuelling demand for homes at inflated prices endures, a consequence of low interest rates in the early decades of the 2000s, and in the aftermath of the 2008 financial crisis, a low interest rate environment engineered through quantitative easing. The crisis in 2008 was itself caused by unrestricted credit, funding speculative investment in housing, leading to unsustainable house price inflation. When interest rates rise and the cost of funding a purchase increases, demand may fall for a period, but in favour of those with capital to put down as a deposit. As unaffordability increases, so demand in the rental sector increases, putting upward pressure on rents. It is a circle of continuing dysfunction.

A market in which supply constantly fails to meet demand is an imperfect one, nevertheless our first consideration should remain, what sort of development builds an environment and community that, for the individuals living in it, promotes health and well-being. Taking a Docklands light railway trip, passing the tall blocks of flats at Plaistow, where once street level community provided support to help neighbours navigate hardship, I am overwhelmed by the spectre of an atomised environment, of high-rise flats literally ungrounded in any notion of healthy, communal living suitable for communities including families with children. It is easy to imagine that in several decades time, when builders' profits have been banked and they have deployed their capital elsewhere, that society will have to confront social ills arising from mass high-level, high-density housing estates, at a great human and financial cost.

When a market is as imperfect as the housing one and seen to function so unfairly, it is easy for the idea of corruption to pervade, so when, as happened in March 2021, a governing political party is paid a donation of £ 150,000, forty eight hours after they approve a controversial housing scheme by the billionaire owner of a property company which made £ 152 million profit in the previous year, the line between market dysfunctionality and perceived corruption is blurred.

The perception that the housing market is inherently flawed is so deep rooted, that in response to a Ministry of Housing report, Lindsay Judge, a senior research and policy analyst at the Resolution Foundation, an organisation representing those on low and middle incomes, acknowledged increasing reliance on parental financial support to finance home ownership. She noted also, that "the underlying drivers of lower home ownership rates, including high prices, are here to stay. As a result, politicians should continue to focus on widespread dissatisfaction with renting and worrying increases in overcrowding".

Reliance on the 'bank of mum and dad' is an indictment of inequality, of opportunity determining quality of life, expectation, and societal connection. This becomes an intergenerational issue, one that embeds inherited, discriminatory economic outcomes. It is commonplace to accept that the underlying causes are "here to stay", conditioned as we are to accept the inevitability of failures associated with the private sector. However, it is not the free market that is to blame, rather our over reliance on the private sector to serve the free market that is the problem.

Once we acknowledge a basic right to an affordable home, just as we should the right to affordable food, we are mandated to be bold and innovate, to find new solutions addressing deep rooted failings in the way our economy functions.

The secondary impact of a dysfunctional housing market is that those who have no option but to rent are obliged to pay rents that are too often beyond affordability. Recent analysis has shown that renters pay £800 more yearly than first time buyers purchasing a three-bedroom home, with the monthly cost of renting rising 10% in a year, compared with 1% for a first-time buyer.[31] If you cannot afford a deposit, or the income to support a home purchase, you pay more as a price for your disadvantage as a renter, the market operates against you.

Approximately a third of income currently, in London significantly more, is taken up by rent in the UK, at which level rent is deemed unaffordable. This is a societal issue, concerning families and children, with 38% of households in the private rented sector having children.[32]

Our existing housing stock is a national, societal asset. There are 25 million existing dwellings in England, and it is forecast that eighty per cent of the housing stock in 2050 has been already built. It is immediately available, and a nationwide resource.

A good measure of societal best interest is the point at which personal and collective self-interest converge. It suits private sector landlords to see rents increase. Indeed, in London, renters are being increasingly required to bid for properties against one another, giving upward momentum to rents, pushing them towards the maximum a renter can afford, or cannot, to secure a home. The self-interest of landlords diverges from that of renters, fracturing society.

A societal form of tenure can change outcomes and by using the existing housing stock, increase the supply of affordable homes to rent, including for specifically targeted groups such as Keyworkers. The self-interest of owner-occupiers seeking income, and renters, requiring affordable tenancies, converges when we incentivise homeowners to create separate, secure, and independent living spaces for tenants at affordable rents. This can be achieved through low cost, reversible, self-financing conversions, with tenancy terms including the provision of shared household services in the rent; lodging or home-share without sharing living space. Personal self-interest in this Homes within Homes programme converges with our collective interest in breaking down the economic divisions which separates us.

Community (Home) Insurance – a better deal for consumers

Risk is either insurable or uninsurable. Often uninsurable risk, cover of last resort, is provided by us collectively. Insurers have traditionally held God responsible for natural, random, dangerous, and damaging events which could not have been foreseen or avoided, where no blame can be assigned to a person. Usually, these "Acts of God" are not excluded from insurance policies, but it all depends on a policy's terms of insurance, and the insurance premium paid by the customer.

Typically, damage due to wind, rain, or hail is covered under standard policy terms but earthquakes, volcanoes and flood are not. This seems fair. Weather is beyond my control, but if I decide to build my home on top of a volcano, on the fault line of the earth's crust, or on a flood plain, risk is in part a consequence of my personal decision. Even if those risks are insurable, they may not be under a standard home insurance policy.

Fire, in my opinion, where no blame attaches to causation, is as good as a random event too. Subsidence is too location specific to be attributable to random acts, and circumstance. Possessions of value, some people acquire them, others not.

We are left with a common risk, faced by all, of loss caused by random, natural events beyond our control, and fire where no blame attaches to its causation. These risks, common to all, may be the only one's I want to insure against. Why then do I have to pay an almost non-negotiable sum for home insurance that far exceeds what is reasonable, with limited excesses, when I would, if able, rather accept higher excesses to keep the premium cost low? In my life I have never encountered anyone who has suffered catastrophic financial loss through a random, no-fault fire risk, although it does occur rarely and when it does it will be devastating. I accept, I may never claim, and that there is a partial contribution I make to pool the risk we face, to our community risk, but should that pooling be inflated by the demand for profit the insurance companies make on me? The market seems 'rigged' against the consumer, no matter how much the insurance industry argues otherwise; it is a conversation I have annually with my insurer as I attempt to defend myself against the standard 8% to 10% increase they always seek to impose. This same pooling of life chances affects individual's financial outcomes in pension planning, between money that belongs to a pension investor, annuity rates and death, between cost, profit, and benefit.

Basic, universal risk, could be pooled through a societised company, purposed to keep the cost of insurance as low as possible for its customers, generating sufficient profit to cover its operating costs and fund its insurable liabilities. Such a company could insure other risks, in competition with privately owned insurers, but its societal goal could be to reshape insurance outcomes in society, by offering the lowest sustainable insurance cost for base risk. A private sector enterprise has no incentive to do this, but a societal one does.

It is a basic, commonly accepted, principle of economics, that producers aim to maximise profits, even if some non-profit purpose attaches to their aims and objectives. Societal enterprise challenges this assumption. Currently, producers seek to maximise profits, and shareholders' wealth, because they are capitalist ventures, privately owned, operating for the benefit of their shareholders, or members. A societal producer, or service provider, may seek to maximise profits, to maximise the contribution it can make using its profit to fund non-profit purpose. Alternatively, it might aim to minimise profit, generating sufficient to fund its business model, but maximising the benefits which are enjoyed by consumers through lower prices, or benefitting other stakeholders, through its decision making.

A human and social citation – a moment to reflect: The Grenfell tragedy, is a human one of pain, loss and suffering beyond insurable value. Seventy-two people lost their lives. Families lost loved ones in a fire, in a tower block covered with flammable cladding. It is reasonable for a building company to keep control of their costs, but a distinction must be made between decisions with no risk, and those exposing residents to risk. The residents of Grenfell were particularly vulnerable, dependent as they were on high rise, public housing. Findings from the first report of the Grenfell Tower inquiry confirmed that the building's exterior did not comply with building regulations. Safety at Grenfell was compromised, with a contractor pocketing a £200,000 saving by using cheap cladding. The government, and construction industry knew about the risks posed by flammable cladding more than a decade before the fire. Private sector companies are susceptible, indeed motivated to cross the line of risk to maximise profit, whether the consequences arise from using inappropriate building materials, or in the case of the 2008 financial crisis, designing complex, inappropriate financial models. That attitude to cost, opportunity, responsibility, and risk can also corrupt the integrity of public service, as indeed it did during the Grenfell refurbishment process. Risk is invariably passed from the private sector to society, at great individual and social cost. That line, of risk is also one of demarcation, between the inherent values of the privately owned corporation, and in contrast, ones defined by the societal good companies can achieve in a societal sector. Bankers discuss with government the need for public, government guarantees on mortgages, and how to deal with firms' liability, and that of individuals if there is a fire in a building with cladding. Separately, a review is taking place about ring-fencing banks activities to protect the public from the avarice of bankers. Control over those who lack common good virtue is a poor substitute to an economy purposed to operate inherently in the public interest.

There is a particular relationship between the societal cost of ill health and addiction, our reliance on the NHS and the caring services, and private sector companies who benefit from activities that can be inherently harmful to good health and well-being.

Gambling is enjoyed by many punters but carries with it the risk of personal harm. The betting industry reaps profit, but there is a personal and social cost to addiction, and over-gambling, caused by its activities. More activity, leads to more profit, leads to greater risk of harm. Harm is measurable through individual suffering, and financially, spending to mitigate adverse social and health impacts. Like the insurance sector, profit is determined by probabilities, odds, and a pooling of risk.

According to accounts published at Companies House, the boss of Bet365, Denise Coates, took home a record £ 469 million pay packet, taking her total pay since 2016 to £ 1.3 billion.[33] On average each of Bet 365s six million customers has therefore gifted £78 to Denise. This is acceptable in the private sector, a reward for entrepreneurship and ability. However, look at the nature of the gambling market from a societal perspective, and what one observes is a market where punters, consumers, pool their money in a game of calculated chance, with the odds literally stacked against them so that there are fewer winners than losers. Shareholders can cream off a sizeable profit margin, which they can extract from the punters through odds and the management of probabilities. Like the insurance market, an individual cannot assess risk which has a pooling characteristic, individual event outcomes appear random, and unpredictable, but can be collectively quantified with certainty over the long-term; the individual consumer is at a disadvantage to the company who profit from this feature of the market.

A societal betting company could operate to pool funds, returning more to punters than a privately owned company can, and its profit could be used for societal purposes, including those directed to the support and well-being of gamblers, rather than rewarding shareholders. Let the consumers, punters decide whether they wish to bet with a company pooling their bets, and paying out the maximum sustainable amount of winnings, consistent with their non-profit societal objectives, or one which withholds pay-outs, to fund dividends and shareholder gains.

Cannabis – prices at cost for the NHS, profits for social use

There are organised distribution chains providing Cannabis, a class B substance, for those who choose to use it recreationally, despite its illegality for this purpose. The Home Office estimate that around a third of 16- to 59-year-olds, some 10 million adults, in England and

Wales, report having used cannabis in their lifetime, with 7.4% (2.4 million) having used the drug in a single year.

The proportion of young adults, between the age of 16 to 24 years age, having used cannabis is estimated to have been 16.2% in the year ending June 2022.[34] Imagining every major Premiership and EFL stadium full beyond capacity with these younger cannabis users, helps visualise the scale of the drug's use.

The drug has been approved for medical use, in 2018, though its use is strictly regulated.

The issues surrounding cannabis use, its legality or prohibition are many and complex. Its features include discriminatory enforcement behaviour around prevention and control, with half of all stop and searches having been linked to suspicion of drug possession. Black people are nine times more likely to be stopped and searched than white people[35], and are 1.4 times more likely to receive an immediate custodial sentence for drug offences than a white offender. For Asian offenders, and those designated "other ethnic groups", the figure is even higher, 1.5 times.[36]

There is a personal and societal cost to the use of cannabis, as there is with alcohol and tobacco. Mental or behavioural disorders linked to cannabis have increased, evidenced by increasing A&E admissions.[37] Dr Marta Di Forti has contributed groundbreaking research into the link between cannabis and psychotic disorders and cognitive capabilities and expresses concern about the effect cannabis has on them.[38] There is no recognised measure of THC comparable to that of units of alcohol helping us determine toxicity and enabling us to make informed choices about its use. THC, tetrahydrocannabinol, is the marijuana plant's primary component for causing psychoactive effects. The medical benefits are under trial now for a wide range of uses, and may include cancer pain, glaucoma, loss of appetite in people with HIV or Aids and epilepsy in children. It is used to relieve sickness and most notably pain, including that caused by muscle spasms in multiple sclerosis. Recreationally it may help relaxation and in controlled adult use, well-being. In the young it is more likely to lead to psychotic disorders. The positive attributes and negative risks associated with the use of this drug make it a complex, societal issue, with no single answer giving us guidance. Its source of supply raises other societal issues of concern.

Albania has been a major source of this drug. Hannah Lucinda Smith reported in the Times that at its height cannabis exports of £ 3.7 billion were more than double the value of Albania's official exports, with more than half of the cannabis sold on UK streets grown in Albania. That production, she noted, has now been shifted by these Albanian gangs to farms in the UK, often inside suburban homes using trafficked migrants as workers.[39] Boris Jordan, a billionaire who is the Founder Executive Chairman of Curaleaf, a company supplying legally approved cannabis estimates the unregulated global market for cannabis to be worth $ 200 billion. He predicts over time it will be used in many products that we purchase and use daily as the drug is increasingly legalised.

We have a product, cannabis, the nature of which can provide benefits, but with the potential to cause huge personal and social harm. Our NHS has a need for cannabis. Its recreational use is a reality, yet unchecked the quality of the drugs being offered for recreational use may be harmful. Cannabis is distributed through criminal gangs and a drug network that debases our collective being. The private sector, naturally, sees the opportunity to profit from legal supply.

There are many uncertainties about how this market will evolve over time. One thing however is certain, our NHS would benefit from being served by a company, supplying product at low, sustainable prices. It is not in our collective interest to pay a profit margin negotiated through weakness, to a shareholder owned company seeking to maximise profit, when we can establish a societised company producing the very same product. A societal company could serve the NHS and public sector at cost but be able to sell recreational cannabis if or when it is legalised in the UK, and for other legal, commercial purposes at a greater profit. The company could ensure standards of quality, toxicity and THP are maintained. The public will have a source of supply they can trust, with the chains of illegal supply undermined. Profit can be used for societal benefit, including funding the work of the NHS and social programmes alleviating the harm of drug use.

Experience teaches us that the private sector lays claim to profit but passes risk, its costs of failure, or incidental harm onto society. This is an intrinsic feature of a private sector economy, and one we constantly observe. We can add cannabis enterprise to this list, but with foresight we can mitigate the adverse consequences of its use and redirect profits from its supply to serve our common good.

The NHS bears many burdens. In a week when Pfizzer stands accused of exploiting a loophole to increase the price of one of the drugs it supplies the NHS to treat epilepsy by 2,600%, Philip Morris, the tobacco giant, raised its bid to purchase a company which treats respiratory illnesses. The company, which produces Marlboro cigarettes, can see a way to grow profits, by acquiring a company treating the very illnesses that it helped create over many decades through its core activities. The NHS state that every year 78,000 people in the UK die from smoking related illnesses, and many more live with debilitating smoking-related illnesses, increasing the risk of developing more than fifty serious health conditions. Over the ten years, 2011-2020, this single tobacco company generated $76 billion of annual net income, on $ 775 billion global net revenue. Founded in 1847, the company stretches the two-hundred-year arc since the industrial revolution. By private sector metrics this indicates a profitable company, generating stable, strong profits. It is a powerful company in a globalised market economy. But, at what cost in human suffering, through pain suffered and early deaths, and of the financial health costs borne by countries over so many years related to its core, historic activity? From a societal perspective, its success is a measure of the global, universal harm which can affect societies across the globe, if profit corrupts humane purpose. Profit cannot measure the incalculable harm caused by the tobacco industry.

The disconnect between the wealth the company accumulated for shareholders, and the public expenditure, funded by tax and borrowing, to deal with illness arising from the company's activities, is manifestly unjust.

Phillip Morris operates naturally, according to its values and private sector instinct. It is not special to them, for over the same historic arc, since 1847, we suffered an environment calamity which caused an even greater threat to life, in search of ever-increasing profit.

In California, Cannabis taxes amount currently to over $ 1 billion per year, a seemingly huge sum, but it has been argued that when set against the costs associated with its use, partially met in the state's $ 200 billion budget, this level of tax does not provide an overwhelming case for the net financial benefit of legalisation. Why though should society rely on a tax-take when it can benefit 100% from the profitable activities of a societally purposed enterprise sector and economy.

Shareholder owned companies are obliged, to maximise profit for their shareholders, and therefore to minimise the tax they pay. It becomes legitimate for companies to avoid tax in any way possible, to a level in some instances, where governments, having been rendered too weak to stand up to global corporate power, accept a tax take that is unfair by any measure of profit, or sales attributable to business activity falling within their jurisdiction. In a societal sector this is not the case, for the population benefit from the full profit a company generates through its societal purpose and from the tax which the spirit of legislation demands.

There is a range of shareholder owned benefit corporations, organisations generating profit but formed as non-profit charities, companies formed by guarantee, charities, and social non-profit enterprises operating for social purposes. It is important to acknowledge their contribution and contrast their form. Some, like Greenwich Leisure Ltd, trading under the Better trademark, operating under the Co-operative and Community Benefit & Societies Act 2014 as a charity, in its case providing leisure, health and library facilities, prove a societal model, incorporating social non-profit goals, works. However, their differences are significant. The Patagonia group, and Motkraft in Norway, show purer societal models exist and operate successfully. We need the political will, and ideological framework to develop a societal form of enterprise which is as ubiquitous, and natural to adopt in a societal sector, as the shareholder owned company is in the private sector.

Social Care – the enterprise economy, taxation, and public expenditure

A traditional economic view is that the private sector delivers the growth, profits, and activity, the tax on which sustains our public services, with government responsible for keeping borrowing and debt at an acceptable level relative to GDP. This is true but only a half-truth. It is the single greatest virtue used to ennoble capitalism, one that is perpetuated relentlessly. Although it is enterprise that delivers these essential benefits, it need not necessarily be enterprise that is privately owned, it can be societally purposed, owned by perpetual trusts. Overwhelming reliance on the tax paid by the private sector is evidence of the monopoly rights the private sector enjoys over the free-market economy, rather than any inherently benevolent characteristic the private sector possesses.

It is all too easy to frame public expenditure as a necessary evil, draining the good from the private sector, and 'productive' economy, when in fact this is not so. Our economy is societal, with government spending financed overwhelmingly directly by taxes paid by consumers and employees, and by levies and duties paid by consumers. Corporation tax, business rates and taxes on production contributed £104 billion, 14.3% of total central government receipts of £723 billion in 2020/21, compared with £340 billion paid by consumers through VAT and Income tax, under PAYE and self-assessment, amounting to 47% of total receipts.[40] Including employee's national insurance and other taxes on the person it is clear, the state is funded primarily by individuals not business. The fact that employee incomes, like tax, may derive from employment in the private sector arises because of the monopoly the private sector enjoys not because it plays a necessarily unique role funding the state.

In a societal economy, there is concomitance, and accord between enterprise to maximise consumer gains and societal purpose and the general body of the population who finance the state. We conflate business tax with a tax on shareholders, and tax therefore is accorded negative attributes associated with our notion of shareholders as wealth creators, when in fact they are private wealth creators. Tax, like societal purpose in a societal economy is another way of directing common resource for societal benefit.

A societal perspective challenges over-reliance on existing corporate forms and outcomes. It also affects how we conceive the existing framework of virtues, and public expenditure and debt which government use as the levers of state.

The debate and policy response to social care throws a light on some of these issues.

'Care in the community' in the 1980s removed people from institutionalised care homes into the community, by encouraging care at home. The aspiration had merit but was often, primarily a way to reduce the financial cost to councils of running residential homes. The issue for social care practitioners has remained one of quality of care, affecting children, young people, and adults, who need extra support and may have physical, mental health and learning attributes which make life harder to live. There are few people who do not experience physical or mental health difficulties at some point in their life, and if not themselves, of loved ones, friends, or neighbours. There is a wide and complex range of need, met by a diverse range of organisations and professionals, within families and communities. Support may require professional expertise and intensive care. On the other hand, as anyone who has cared for an elderly person with dementia may know, support takes the form, at least in its early stages, of interaction, and help with the basic needs of life, shopping, cooking, cleaning, and washing. This is an issue of common care, a societal issue we share, like health.

We may be able to supplement and assist the professional care sector by promoting care within and of the community through social care contracts linked to a Homes within Homes programme, providing accommodation for those needing care and support. As it is, social care reform has crystallised around financial resource not method and programme. This makes little sense, because it is all but impossible to decide on the level of resource required to fund a programme which has yet to be devised. The Government has introduced a new health and social care levy of 1.25% payable by employees and employers through national insurance, to reduce post-covid hospital waiting times, and then free up any residual money from the tax to fund social care. It protects the assets of older age people, with a cap on care costs falling on each person, limited to £ 86,000 over their lifetime. The government is on course to lift the tax 'burden' to about 35.5% of GDP, taking it to the highest point for more than seventy years.

This additional 1.25% tax on wages paid by employers has been called a "tax on jobs", "a drag on jobs growth" and a disincentive for those who might consider investing in the UK. Tom Danker, the director-general of the CBI at that time, is reported as having been, "deeply worried the government thinks that taxing business is without consequence to growth". He continues, "there is a real risk the government will keep turning to business taxes to carry the load ...... if we want to kick-start the growth capital for the next decade, we should do so by rewarding those businesses who choose to invest". It is paradoxical that having lauded the power of private sector investors, he acknowledges that Britain lags its economic competitors with a relatively lower rate of investment as a proportion of GDP and calls for "catalytic public investment" to draw out private money into investment.[41] This is instinctive mythologising, suggesting that business taxes carry the load when consumers and employees do.

The sledgehammer threat that without a low tax environment for business, investment will be directed elsewhere to maximise shareholder returns is a truth. Like poor relations we hold out our collective begging bowl, when we have the financial and collective strength and resource to create a vigorous, productive economy with sufficient investment, through a mixed economy comprising the private sector, but also a societal one asserting our collective economic power. If we fail to do so, then those nations which have adapted society to capitalism, and build strength through sovereign intervention, wealth management and funds, will secure higher levels of growth and prosperity.

The marginal tax paid on total income by an employee repaying their graduate loan now stands at 41%, comprising 20% basic rate tax, 12% national insurance and 9% student loan repayment, and will rise to 42.25%. After paying half to two thirds of net pay on rent and bills, paid food, and travel costs, little is left to build up a permanent stake in society by building up personal capital, and for those who wish to, eventually buying a home. A graduate employee needs to work to live, a shareholder owned company can choose where to work to maximise profit. This is as it is, this is not as it should or could be, and is an inter-generational issue. Unlike the cap on contributions from the predominantly old, who avoid having to sell properties, there is no cap on contributions into the social care "fund", it is a lifetime societal contribution that each employee will make. However, it is misleading for government to suggest there is a fund, for none exists, with contributions financing current expenditure, made on the understanding that future generations will support today's young as they age, just as they do those in later life currently.

We are told constantly, as the CBI reminded us when employer's national insurance was increased to help fund social care, that business requires a low tax regime to incentivise it and its investment. Need as ever is a lever used by those in power to motivate people to work, gain to motivate those with the ability and opportunity to increase shareholder wealth.

The graduate employee I refer to above may well have lived in student accommodation provided by a private sector company. Unite Group, which focuses on supporting students and goals beyond profit maximisation, do just that and in the six months ended June 2021, reported a

£ 130.4 million pre-tax profit for their shareholders. This company may operate with virtuous principles of governance and purpose, yet, on average each of their 74,000 beds will have contributed £ 1,762 towards the company's profit after its operating costs, an annualised figure more than £ 3,500 per student. Unite Group cannot be criticised for making a profit for shareholders, but it remains that a societal company could operate for its consumer's, student's best interest. By operating to keep rent costs as low as possible, an enterprise operating for this core societal purpose could charge lower rents, saving students up to £ 10,000 over the duration of their degrees.

Energy – a societal response to the costs of living

We cannot rely on private sector 'competition' to lead to best price, so Ofgem, an industry regulator, caps the tariffs that energy companies can charge customers. In August 2021 the cap was increased allowing energy companies to charge more. Consumers can expect to pay higher prices to fund hydrogen growth, to pay for decarbonisation, including the construction of new nuclear energy plants, and higher prices for food, goods, and travel to reduce the impact of polluting industries. These costs will total many hundreds of pounds for most consumers over the coming years, as we attempt to move towards a low carbon economy. Lest we forget, the foundation of private capital which lays claim to market profits now, was built up over many decades in a high carbon environment.

This week, at the time of writing, when dozens of electricity companies face collapse, the energy market is in crisis.

Gas supplies forty per cent of energy consumption, and the wholesale price of gas has increased, as has demand following the recovery from covid, lower than usual supplies from Russia, and more liquefied natural gas being delivered to Asia. The wholesale price has increased sixfold in the past year and doubled in the last two months. The price cap which limits the prices energy companies can charge has restricted their ability to increase prices. Nevertheless, prices will increase immediately for those having to change supplier if their current one ceases trading, and prices in the longer term will increase as the price cap allows suppliers to increase standard tariffs by 12% in October 2021, affecting eleven million households on a standard variable tariff, and four million, often the poorest, with prepayment meters.

The government has stepped in, underwriting loans supporting energy companies in distress, and it is likely that consumers will pay more as these loans are repaid. An unforeseen consequence of the rise in energy costs follows the decision of CF Industries, an American privately owned company, to cease production at its fertiliser plant because of the high energy cost, leading to a chronic undersupply of CO_2, a biproduct of fertiliser production, used in the food industry. Tens of millions of pounds is being given to CF Industries in subsidy to encourage them to start production and avoid food shortages in what the Prime Minister has called "a unique circumstance". These conditions may be unique, but grants and bailouts of the private sector by government are commonplace. Food shortages were of no meaningful concern to CF Industries when it made its decision to cease production, it had no societal responsibility.

Energy, food, and housing are essentials and their availability, and the amount consumers are charged is a significant determinant of their cost of living. Government has constructed a substantial regulatory structure to protect consumers and society from injurious or anti-competitive behaviour, and the cap on energy prices is one such mechanism. This is a poor substitute for a market which is inherently more competitive and works for consumers best interest in the first place. If the energy sector included companies working for societal objectives, providing energy to its customers at the lowest sustainable prices, then the energy market could be perfected in favour of consumers, helping lower their cost of living, and reduce energy poverty, without solely relying on Ofgem. To see purposeful enterprise working with this outcome may appear to many to be too idealistic, showing a naïve understanding of how business works. Yet, in Norway, a company founded by a group of students in Norway, Motkraft, is doing just that. It supplies energy at cost and earns sufficient profit to cover its operating costs through low, fixed charges. The model exists, we just need to embrace its full potential.

The shortage of CO_2 means the price may rise fivefold. When added to other pressures, producers are warning currently that food prices may rise. Consumers are facing increases in the cost of their living, with the Monetary Policy Committee of the Bank of England forecasting that inflation may reach "above 4 per cent into the second quarter of 2022".[42] This understated the scale of the cost-of-living crisis, with consumer prices during the twelve months ended June 2023 rising 7.9%, and food prices by 17.4%.

The foundational issue flowing from this societal cost, that of living, paid by the general population is: should an economy be systemised to maximise profit for shareholders, or reformed, to minimise the cost of living for consumers through non-shareholder owned enterprises? Economic theory is founded on the principle that profit, leads to productivity and is one part of a production supply equation with consumers sitting on the demand side of the fence. This need not be so, indeed should not be so; an economy can just as well be productive, grow and be organised to minimise prices for consumers.

Governments have the power to invest, they merely choose to do it to support the private sector, rather than developing a societal sector which benefits the public generally. The British Business Bank was established by government to use public funds to support investment in UK-based companies, provided private investors match its funding. It facilitated the Future Fund. The Fund is now closed. The fund supported an education start-up, Mrs Wordsmith, but the enterprise failed six months after public funds were invested in it, and the 'taxpayer' is likely to recover only £ 40,000 of its £ 650,000 investment. The total cost borne collectively is higher because the company received grants of public money through the furlough scheme. One of the minority shareholders in Mrs Wordsmith was Catamaran Venture Uk, a private investment vehicle. Following the failure of the business it has been bought out of insolvency by a Monaco-based hedge fund tycoon. It has been reported that the company was on the brink of failure when public funds were committed to it. Companies successfully having navigated covid and supported by the scheme are returning to full private ownership.[43] One can applaud entrepreneurial enterprise and accept the need for government to invest in the enterprise economy, but our reduced notion of enterprise, public expenditure and rights attaching to collective, public investment should not preclude the sustained development of societal wealth, through societal ownership, and an opening up of the free market to greater competition through non-private sector companies. The state-owned British Bank has published a list of 158 companies in which the "taxpayer", better described as society, hold shares, through the Future Fund, indicating that where there is a will for government to invest, there is a way. If government invests in this way to assist the private sector, then it can do so to develop a societal sector benefitting the general population and the nation directly.

A societal response to housing need can help increase affordable housing. A societised food retailer can operate to reduce the effects of food poverty. Societised drugs and pharmaceutical companies could help finance health and social care provision. Consumers standard of living can be improved through societised insurance. Decarbonisation can be effected through societised energy companies, rewarding consumers through lower prices for the duties and levies they are obliged to pay to meet the challenge of climate change. The transformational possibilities which flow from a societal economy, for consumers and society's benefit, are endless.

Private equity constantly "runs the rule" over UK companies, a product of mergers and acquisition activity to maximise privatised wealth, not to meet societal need. It is time for society and politicians, claiming to represent its best interest, to begin running the rule over the market economy.

Chapter 4

POLITICS and ECONOMY –
Re-engagement, Representation and Responsibility

To live in one land is captivity, To run all
countries a wild roguery.
Waters stink soon, if in one place they bide,
And in the vast sea are more putrified;
But when they kiss one bank, and leaving this
Never look back, but the next bank do kiss,
Then they are the purest; change is the nursery
Of music, joy, life and eternity

John Donne[44]

A covid introduction

When I received my first covid vaccine jab, a third of the population in the UK had been given at least one dose of vaccine. Across the planet, far fewer had enjoyed the comfort of vaccination. The human cost of covid, in lives lost and reduced, of death for too many and lesser life chances for the living, had been dramatic, sad, and brutal.

The sun shone brightly, the early Spring air and its green shoots gave a sense that warmer and happier days lay ahead of us. The ground I ran over before my jab was slightly firmer. I could feel the change in season.

Several years ago, my mother was living with dementia in a care home. One day, early in December, she touched her glasses and they shifted from her nose to somewhere between cheek and ear, crooked, lopsided. She shrugged and smiled gently, and in that moment we both new that her dementia was what it was, and there was little we could do about it. As I left her room, she shouted to Sarah and me, "see you soon". We did not see her again, for she died the following morning. This is not a sad reminiscence, it is a recognition that there are moments when a part of us is touched in a way that goes to the heart of who we are, an emotional and human link beyond words.

My vaccine expedition touched me too, impeccably organised, handled with a purposeful sense of urgency, we were admitted, jabbed and back intact, sitting in an observation room within five minutes of arrival. The staff, a mixture of practitioners, professionals, and volunteers, shepherded, checked, and guided us and I felt grateful. Without time to truly thank and praise my helpers, it was over, by then I was a meaningful statistic as they moved on to the next group of vaccine seekers. This was a society in action, working for our collective well-being. Covid remains a moment from which to learn something about ourselves, touching on the deepest issues of how we should live.

We were led 'by the science' during the covid pandemic, necessarily advised, ordered, and behaviourally manipulated by government, but we took our inspiration from community activism, motivated as much by heart as reason, and the reasoned demands we made on behalf of those we knew were working on our behalf, particularly the NHS staff.

The essence of this collective spirit was captured by Captain Sir Tom Moore who, with his hundredth birthday approaching, decided to raise money for the NHS, walking, with the aid of his frame, one hundred lengths of his twenty-five-metre garden. He explained that "the doctors and nurses, they're all on the front line, and all of us behind, we've got to supply them and keep them going with everything they need". This was a devotion for community, a simple, sincere, selfless, personal act of duty. It was at one with the weekly hand clapping from homes, a reaching out to friends and neighbours as much as a recognition of the valuable work NHS staff were doing. The values which drove Captain Sir Tom were understood by all, shared by most, a manifestation of working in unity to meet society's needs at a time of crisis. It is not beyond our ambition to devise a system that incorporates similar unifying, collective aspirations, and values into our mixed economy so that everyday economic life can be something we participate in for each other's interdependent common good. The strength of societal expectation drove government policy where it needed to go, often against the governments first wishes, and demanded a fair template for social lockdown and restrictions.

Beyond the instinctive, natural values we shared, a societal force promoting our collective well-being, the ones fostered by Captain Sir Tom, there was a sense that a partnership between the private sector, government and the people had worked successfully during covid, an extraordinary alliance facing an exceptional crisis. Despite many failings along the way, death rates, hospital admissions and infection rates fell, economic activity improved, and a road map to national health and economic recovery established. There was also a much stated ambition, and hope, that after covid we can organise our affairs in a fairer way, that "'things' should not remain the same", that by government and the private sector collaborating and targeting sectors leading to economic growth, we can frame a future with greater prosperity in a post-Brexit world, anticipating that this model of co-operation and direction will enable us to manage growth so that a levelling up agenda could be achieved. Whether or not this is true, or achievable is not at issue, the essence of our covid experience shows that we operate at our best when we unify around collective, shared purpose. This is how our economy can function.

In the early days of the covid pandemic, in the UK, a shortage of personal protective equipment gave government a mandate to employ the private sector to increase the availability of this much needed, essential supply. Unprepared and with no other supply channels available to use, it could do little else but rely on private sector personal initiative, of business owners motivated by profit and undoubtedly for many by social concern too. It appeared that a government sponsored gold rush had arrived; provided you had a contact, often someone from the political class, you could enter the dash for public cash and PPE. It worked at a huge cost, and because the public knew front-line workers were desperate for protection, process and cost became of little concern. However, this is not how a system of economy should work, not even in a crisis.

The nexus between Government and the private sector and the state's reliance on the private sector is so great that public service ethical values of independence, accountability, transparency, competence, efficiency, objectivity, and trust are compromised. It has led to conflicts of interest. This was epitomised during the government procurement process during covid.

The convoluted yet embedded links between the private sector and government have been shown to extend to the civil service. David Cameron, a former Prime Minister, had multi-million-pound share options in the failed company Greensill Capital and used his government contacts to try to persuade government officials, including the then Chancellor Rishi Sunak, to use public funds to finance the company. The same company employed a senior civil servant, the government's former chief commercial officer, who simultaneously worked for a time for the government while also advising the board of Greensill Capital. Lex Greensill himself, the founder of the supply chain finance company that bears his name, described by Cameron as a "refreshing" newcomer in the world of fintech, technology supporting financial services, secured himself a Cabinet Office desk through the civil servant Jeremy Heywood.

These interconnected links have always existed, and personal interest manifested irrespective of party. Power and the opportunity for personal gain can corrupt process.

Personal failing is inevitable, but governance built around a system that encourages personal ambition, but also entrenches public service values for collective, social purpose can counter-balance the prevailing dominance and power of the private sector and its creed of unfettered personal financial self-interest.

The financial assistance given through the covid furlough scheme, help to the self-employed, business rates relief, bounce back loans and other support has been essential, yet tells us little of systemic significance. Governments do not have an independent resource, they use social capital and public money, taken or borrowed, and financed currently or by shifting the costs from one generation to another, for their purposes and always have.

However, the reliance on the public purse and resource compels us to design a system that commensurately, intrinsically, and inherently benefits the public. Justice demands that if society collectively bears costs, it should be able to assert rights and claim rewards. A payback time comes, particularly after the 2008 financial crisis, and the costs the public endured because of it, and most recently the covid crisis. It makes reform a matter for today not tomorrow.

The collaboration, during covid, between government, responsible for national good health, Oxford University, expert in vaccinology, and Astra Zeneca, a global pharmaceutical company with a technical and productive capability, presented a way enterprise can operate beyond traditional boundaries.

Astra Zeneca reported $ 26.6 billion total revenue in 2020, with an operating profit of $ 5.2 billion, $ 4.8 billion of net cash flow and $ 3.6 billion of dividends. Leif Johansson, the company's chairman, reported that the decision to develop and supply the vaccine at no profit during the pandemic "was not taken lightly". He says the decision "brings scrutiny to what we do and how we do it".[45] The Anglo-Swedish company can be applauded for selling the vaccine without a profit margin. However, they may have had little real choice; had covid become a profitable business proposition for Astra Zeneca, the UKs lead supplier of vaccine, then the strength of the crisis pact between government and people may have been weakened or broken. It did not break, because we felt, and indeed were, 'in it all together'. Astra's decision to supply the vaccine at no profit was within its gift. Society benefited through their social purpose and patronage, but not as of right. Had the company decided to profit from supplying the vaccine there was little anyone could do.

Moderna and Pfizer, Astra Zeneca's American cousins decided to sell the vaccine on a commercial basis. Astra too benefited financially but in an indirect and less visible way. As Moderna's second largest shareholder, holding 7.7% of the company, Astra Zeneca made a substantial profit from selling its stake in the company after the

American biotechnology's company's shares soared on the back of its coronavirus vaccine breakthrough. Moderna's shares surged from $ 29 to peak at $ 186 within a year, its valuation transformed by its success using mRNA technology in its design of an effective covid vaccine.

The reason why Astra Zeneca's decision not to profit from supplying its covid vaccine is deemed both natural and admirable, is that at that moment of decision, for a fleeting moment, in just one aspect of its business, it wore the clothes of a societal company, working at one with society's collective will for our common good.

Politics and societism

Politicians have the privilege of power, and with power comes responsibility, not only to craft policy in accordance with their manifestos, for the good of party and country, but also to preserve the integrity of our democracy.

To fully represent society, and remain engaged with the population, politicians should represent the breadth, not only of current opinions within the nation, but also more deeply, of our diverse ideologies and values. This can take place in three ways, first by parliament being comprised of members of parliament, selected by our political parties, who represent our societal diversity fully. However, the party machine, whip, and allegiance militate against individual politicians making parliament a plural institution.

A structural view of representative plurality in parliament relies therefore primarily on the reform of our election voting system, to erode the dominance of our two main political parties in favour of multi-party governance, through proportional representation. The hope for many is that consensual decision making, rather than belligerent opposition, will lead to better policy.

The second way in which greater plurality can be achieved, is not through electoral process, but the emergence of new ideas, threads of alternative ideology or ideas which permeate the policy making of parties without necessarily requiring a political realignment or change in the composition of parliament. Electoral success relies on 'reaching out', often beyond the boundaries of existing ideology, a place where party members' views must connect with the broader populace, which compels parties to refine their message and policy. Yet, reaching out is too often a short-term re-positioning based on electoral advantage, rather than rooted in foundational values.

The third way pluralism could be injected into our body politic is through foundational ideological adaptation. It is particularly relevant to the Liberal Democratic Party and the Labour Party, the former not having been a majority administration for over a century and the other having been in office for only a little over 30% of the period since 1979, none whatsoever since 1979 if the Blair and Brown governments are excluded, and a little less than 40% since 1945. Both parties need to reassess the fundamental reasons for their electoral failure at national level.

It is over a hundred years since ideology drove significant political realignment, dating back to the last majority

Liberal government under Asquith, who served as Prime Minister from 1908 to 1916. The Liberals, an alliance of Whigs, free traders, and radicals, was one of the two major parties, opposing the other, the Conservative Party, in the 19th and early 20th centuries. Often on the right side of history and social change, the Liberals inhabited undefined territory, with no ideological identity of seeming relevance when politics became polarised between Conservative capitalism and Labour's socialism, particularly once the Iron Curtain had subsequently descended.

Values and virtues do not amount to an ideological identity, and without one the Liberals place as the main opposition to Conservatism was supplanted by Labour and has remained so to this day.

Politics drove the structure of our economy; the economy dictates our daily and electoral political cycle. Economic justice is unlikely to be achieved unless systemic economic reform is attached to political, ideological renewal. For the Lib Dems this is an existential issue, one not properly addressed for over a century, for the Labour Party it may become of equal importance. Societism, the politics of representing society as a distinct, identifiable economic entity is an ideology which propels pluralism to the heart of parliament and our democracy. Its advocacy into the political mainstream will require engagement, effort, courage, and vision.

The Labour Party

What would the Labour Party look like, what ideology would inform its policy, indeed would it even exist as the main opposition party if we did not have a first past the post electoral system in the UK? That system, often referred to as a plurality system to distinguish it from a system of preferential voting, leads to a far from plural parliament.

The Labour Party has a rich ideological heritage, founded in 1900, a product of socialist intellectual ideology and trades union activism to improve the working conditions of employees. This union, represented by the Labour Party in parliament, has remained a counterpoise to capitalism, asserting collectivist, public welfare and individual employee and social rights largely through state intervention and regulation, and using the reforming power of legislation. The coalition of interest groups, networks, and its party structure, embodying its collaborative strength, however, incites internal controversy, often in search of its 'soul' and fidelity to its roots.

At the first night of a Labour Conference at Brighton, in 1981, in a darkened room at the Royal Pavilion, the Labour Herald was hosting the first fringe meeting of the week. The deputy leadership contest was to take place between Dennis Healey and the more left-wing Tony Benn. There was a lot of heckling and shouting, David Blunkett made an impassioned call for tolerance, between individuals caught up in a struggle between right and left for control of the Party. The heckling and sincere, self-righteous rage continued, year in year out, as it had done for previous decades.

In 1985, Neil Kinnock dispatched Derek Hatton, the deputy leader of Liverpool City Council and Militant, a

Trotskyist grouping following Marxist beliefs, with his 'reality check', accusing them of causing "grotesque chaos". He repositioned the membership so that eventually Tony Blair could take Labour to power in 1997, after which the Labour Party enjoyed thirteen years in majority government at Westminster. The voice of Militant in the eighties was supported by Jeremy Corbyn, who with, and through Momentum, fought a similar battle for control of the Labour Party, culminating in Labour's defeat in the 2019 General Election.

The choice that Jeremy Corbyn gave the electorate was clear and identifiable, the traditional, entrenched bi-polar options of capitalist Conservatism, or a self-declared socialist alternative referred to popularly as Corbynism. The Corbynist 'socialist' party, a logical offering for a party influenced by Momentum to make, was however vague in how it would manage an economy reliant on private enterprise, giving no systemic nor credible vision of an alternative system, instead just the tried and less than trusted ideas for management of the economy based on intervention, tax, and redistribution. The Labour Party's failure to embrace new ideas expressing their core beliefs, within a framework of economy that attaches to those beliefs, exposes them to the same risks the Liberal Party failed to address, leading to marginalisation and electoral irrelevance at national level over the long-term. Of seeking to manage capitalism to give precisely the outcomes for the collective good that are inherently absent from it, an impossible task.

It was quite proper for there to have been an enduring internal debate within the Labour Party about the meaning and relevance of its socialist identity, for policy and organisation. However, the interconnected allegations of entryism, of parties within a party, subverted this legitimate discussion into energy sapping, febrile battles for power within the party. A discussion leading to ideological renewal would have been meaningful, as it was, this was not possible, with its terms of reference rooted in the party's history, not its future. Tony Blair was a proponent of the third way, a social democratic repositioning seeking compromise and synthesis between the different factions within the Labour Party, based on a centre-right economic platform and centre-left social policy. For an electorate starved of a clear appeal to the values of the Centre this was an ideological shift sufficient for the Labour Party to win three elections, but it was inadequate to reconcile the internal divisions within the Party over belief. The inherent contradictions of a political party confused by its socialist heritage, coming to terms with a global economy that is capitalist and accepted to be so by the electorate has been disastrous, for both Party and the people it aspires to represent.

Socialism had its time and place, without it much needed reform and representation would not have taken place. However, it is now part of an old-world order which needs to be challenged and reshaped. The path for the Labour Party is clear, fail to adapt ideology, as the Liberals failed over a hundred years ago and it is likely Conservatism will continue to prevail, largely unchallenged, enjoying ideological hegemony over the economy.

Most politicians are well intentioned, working tirelessly for their constituents and the wards they represent. Ideology comes second to the day-to-day work of representation, and resolving problems their constituents present to them. Republicans in the US can be heard taunting Democrats, referring to them as "socialists". I have observed similar ideological cat calling, of Conservative councillors branding Labour members as "socialists", in council chamber meetings, a mixture of parody and denunciation, an accusation of irrelevance. They had a point, because during a fifty-year period when Labour should have been arming itself with an understanding of societal change, and adapting its ideology to increase its electoral credibility, it did not do so. The lady whose iron was partially forged in that same local political establishment, Margaret Thatcher, a proponent of neo-liberalist economic policy and laissez-faire capitalism, had an open goal to shoot at, and Conservatism still does. Labour may be rewarded with greater electoral success if it crafts an ideological response appealing to the electorate's intrinsic sense of fairness and equity.

Conservatism

Does an identifiably distinct societist reference point, its language and construction, have any relevance to the Conservative Party? Perhaps not, the Party, resolutely adhering to the economics of the individual and market are the predominant force in British politics. They enjoy the position of a party whose ideology is a political expression of our economy, umbilically and symbiotically connected to it. To espouse Conservatism is to champion the supremacy of a private sector comprising companies owned by shareholders, and to build the economy and society around that capitalist value system.

An economy that is not exclusively dominated by privately owned enterprise would, I suspect, be anathema for most Conservatives. For electorally justified reasons, Conservative's share a conviction, commonly accepted by the general population, that private sector capitalism is the only credible driver for a successful economy. The reward for this is political primacy. However, Conservative policy bends towards society, in economic terms this has recently been called 'levelling up', using conventional levers of tax, borrowing, and spending to improve regional equality. In economy Conservatism does not embrace market societism, in its politics it embraces a societal agenda to connect with the electorate.

The levelling up agenda is characterised by regional economic disparity, action to improve the economic welfare of relatively, and absolutely, disadvantaged areas, and an electoral analysis of the politics of this issue. Too often, politicians and commentators harness perceptions of societal difference to the cause of levelling up. This is divisive. In a market economy there are limits to what can be achieved through spending and redistribution, there are too many forces which determine wealth and the location of business, nevertheless government intervention to ensure regional equality remains important.

Ameliorative redistribution achieves some re-balancing but not enough. The government announced a £ 4.8 billion levelling-up fund for infrastructure and transport development, whilst the full cost, to level up productivity, economic, health and educational outcomes and life expectancy has been estimated by Paul Swinney, policy director at the Centre for Cities, to be comparable to the cost of German reunification. This is estimated at some £ 2 trillion, more than half of which was spent on welfare, unemployment support and pensions.[46] Societal enterprise can operate for a range of purposes including those associated with levelling up, using the full resource of profit to help train and improve the skill levels necessary to achieve regional growth, and prosperity. The aims and purposes of enterprise can be redirected to the regions when shareholder value may not justify it. Societisation enables us to assert objectives beyond growing shareholder wealth, including those of regional significance.

You cannot 'buck' the markets is a much vaunted aphorism, and applies to regional investment based on risk, return and cost. It is true in many respects, but the extent of that truth depends on how a market operates, according to the objectives of those serving and being served by it. Our reductionist view of what an enterprise economy can be has led us towards a diminished view of how political power can be exercised for our collective well-being.

The Labour Party has failed to reconcile its foundational ideology, its identity, with the reality of an economic system that is capitalist. It has spent decades trying to do so through its internal battles over identity, which prevails the red rose or the red flag? It has failed to embrace the mixed economy by devising an economic system which embodies its belief values, a failure of vision. Conservatism on the other hand, buttressed by the certainties the current economic system gives it, is inevitably drawn towards the self-interest of the individual, with potentially insufficient regard for societal well-being. This has implications for Conservatism in the modern era.

A Conservative view of society was definitively expounded by Margaret Thatcher. In 1987; she said:

.... there is no such thing as society. "There are individual men and women and there are families. And no government can do anything except through people, and people must look after themselves first. It is our duty to look after ourselves and then, also, to look after our neighbours".[47]

She was talking about people relying on government to solve their problems, specifically referring to homelessness, and reliance on government to provide housing.

Whether you agree or disagree with her statement, what resonates is a legitimate, honest, and revealing avowal of a view of society which is consistent with advocacy of an economy built on principles of individualism and private gain through the private sector. For her, selfishness inspires and motivates, which it can, but it assumes personal self-interest leads to the best collective outcomes. However, too often society is fractured by the divergence of personal self-interest and societal well-being. A societal economy and the political ideology which underpins it, commands the following injunction, "yes, there is such a thing as society", and more than that, "society is best served through the convergence of personal and collective self-interest in a societal economy".

In the same interview, Mrs Thatcher said, "I think we have gone through a period when too many children and people have been given to understand, 'I have a problem, it is the Government's job to cope with it!' or 'I have a problem, I will go and get a grant to cope with it!' 'I am homeless, the Government must house me!' and so they are casting their problems on society and who is society? There is no such thing!".

Mrs Thatcher in this statement of foundational values, betrays the untruth we have not dared to challenge with sufficient vigour, that capitalism and individualism lead to a natural form of economy, mirroring our basic human nature. She also betrays the truth, that society is currently not recognised as a distinct political and economic entity. It should be. Although, Mrs Thatcher's words were spoken forty years ago, they are still relevant, a statement of a paradigm that still exists, and binds us to the past.

Her view of society fits a traditional view of economy, based on the individual and the individual within family, community, and state. Society is deemed to be one more component to which the individual attaches. However, society is to the individual in social and economic community, what the private sector is to the share owning investor in the business community.

Mrs Thatcher saw individual need as unnecessarily and unreasonably dependent on the state, preferring to see people stand on their own two feet, seemingly oblivious to the fact that her preferred system of economy depends systemically on society and the state underwriting its failures to meet that need. Second, individuals suffer the problems she identifies, including homelessness, because of inherent failings in the system she advocated. If government abrogates responsibility for providing homes, as Mrs Thatcher did, then they must ensure markets operate so people can find homes themselves, without relying on the state.

We all know that if NHS workers had put self-first, reduced their risk of exposure to the covid virus to protect themselves, and those they loved, then we, as a society, would have suffered far greater during the covid pandemic; they did not. They understood there are societal responsibilities beyond personal self-interest and make professional oaths making patients health their primary concern. It could be argued that the context of Mrs Thatcher's statement was economic, not social, but herein lays the essence of market societism, it unifies the economy and society through convergent interest.

Mrs Thatcher's view of governmental irresponsibility is shared by the former Prime Minister Boris Johnson. In the face of potential food shortages, arising in part from a lack of hauliers, rising energy prices, and other supply chain issues, in the autumn 2021, he told business leaders that avoiding Christmas food shortages is their responsibility and it is not the government's job to fix supply problems. For good measure the Foreign Secretary underlined the message, saying the Prime Minister should escape blame even if people are unable to buy what they want at Christmas.

The conundrum that both Mrs Thatcher and Boris Johnson present to us goes to the heart of the need for societal economic reform. They suggest government cannot intervene. Mrs Thatcher places responsibility back onto the individual. Mr Johnson places responsibility back onto the private sector. There is merit in the argument that government should not intervene to cure all the ills of the private sector. However, what then is the solution to problems arising from over-reliance on the private sector when it fails us? If government is not to intervene to protect individuals from market failures, who is? Unless we accept the hopeless position that markets will fail us, and burdens must be endured, society must be granted the rights to make markets work where the private sector fails. Far from there being no such thing as society, it is only society which can carry the weight of our social need, by being granted equal access to markets to make them work as they should, for our collective economic benefit.

Neo-liberalism demands less state intervention to make markets 'freer', yet that freedom for capitalists to operate, unfettered by any social obligation, to maximise shareholder wealth, causes greater need for the state to intervene to protect the general population from capitalism's inherent failings. This is a significant paradox. Those who oppose neo-liberalism, too readily conflate their opposition to those liberalist economic values, with the markets themselves, often seen as central to problems associated with unconstrained capitalism. It suits neo-liberalists to diminish the terms of reference of this debate, encouraging reformists not to look beyond a capitalist framework.

Market outcomes do not necessarily serve our collective best interest. Neo-liberalists seek outcomes that increasingly serve private best-interests. However, it is not the markets but the ethics of people purposing business, which serve markets, that determines their impact. Capitalism's most ardent purists will always argue for less state intervention, which those who believe in collective best interest must challenge. However, the paradigm leap requires us to challenge our preconceptions and reframe the debate. Neo-liberalists seek to liberalise markets, making them freer, to maximise personal wealth through the private sector. Reformists must liberate markets for the public good, freeing them up through increasing competition and plurality, making them more democratic through a societal sector.

Conservatism faces a choice; to coalesce around a pro-capitalist ideology guided by a moral social compass, to follow a path towards neo-liberalism, deregulation, and a low tax economy, or it could broaden its ideological base, through threads of market societism of electoral relevance to our modern age.

Liberal Democacy

The Liberal Democrats are a conundrum. A party whose values are undeniably shared by many, cannot mobilise sufficient electoral support in the centre ground of politics to either 'break the mould of British politics', to govern, or form the main opposition party in parliament. In contrast Tony Blair and the politicians supporting his beliefs within the Labour Party succeeded by appealing to a similar centre ground coalition, winning power in three successive general elections and becoming Labour's longest serving Prime Minister.

In the Preamble to their Constitution Lib Dem values are stated clearly, that the party exists, 'to build and safeguard a fair, free and open society' and champion, the freedom, dignity and well-being of individuals, balancing values of liberty, equality, and community. The Lib Dem's commitment, societist in all but name, is to 'foster a strong, sustainable economy which encourages necessary wealth creation processes', one that works 'for the benefit of all, with a just distribution of the rewards of success'. Is this, however, a statement of values and aspirations rather than an ideological identity. More important do the public understand who the Lib Dems are, other than being "neither of the other two parties".

The Lib Dems are an individualistic party, eschewing collectivism, and ideological adherence to any "–ism".

This is an authentic response, implicitly recognised in their constitution, and connects with the role of their membership to local activism and in policy formation. It was also a natural path to follow when the dividing line in British politics was between market capitalism and socialism, but not now.

There are three outcomes for all Lib Dem members and their Party to contemplate. The first, which should also be a major concern for the Labour Party, is that the Conservative Party and their vision of a mixed economy based on private ownership prevails, unchallenged. This implies little change in electoral fortune, and economic and social outcomes flowing directly from the economic system. However, doing nothing but maintaining the status quo brings with it the certainty, and uncertainties, of stasis, and allows political parties to re-tread, familiar, and in the short term, less demanding paths.

The second outcome is that one or other, or both of the historical leading opposition parties, Labour and the Liberal Democrats seek to revitalise their electoral standing through ideological renewal, establishing a discernible and clear identity which expresses their core beliefs, and values which goes beyond identity, to their establishment ego.

The Labour Party elevates ideology, but in its confusion about the true, modern relevance of that ideology, its identity and the values attaching to it can lack authenticity and credibility, attributes necessary to win trust. The Liberal Democrats have certainty in the values that imbue their Party, but because they eschew ideology, they lack an identity that projects their Party to the electorate, in a clear and meaningful way. Conservatism, certain, authentic and appearing credible governs largely unchallenged. The parties of opposition need to be seen as authentic, clear, credible, and enabled to be bold and confident, allied to a system that operates to their value system, as uniquely and identifiably as capitalism does to the Conservative Party. The politics and economics of societal best interest are simple, clear, credible, and identifiably unique.

The historian Thomas Bartlett contextualises the impact of the 1916 Easter rebellion on the Irish Party and the Liberal Party with simple, and brutally true words, he writes, "the Irish (Parliamentary) Party, like the Liberal Party, had been conceived in gentler times: neither could function, let alone flourish, in an era of total war: and both were ultimately to be consigned to the dustbin of history".[48] Value driven, political liberalism could not survive in a world divided ideologically between capitalists and socialists, especially in the UK with its first-past-the-post, single member, electoral system for the House of Commons, and unelected, second chamber. However Liberal democratic values, attached to the double-edged ideological rapier, of political societal well-being and economic market societism could cut through to the electorate. It restores the gentler politics of values to which Thomas Bartlett refers, attaching them to a kinder, but nevertheless radical, reformist agenda that can flourish in these more peaceful times.

For those, particularly the many within the Labour Party who stand by its socialist credentials and heritage, the radicalism of societal claims for the common good find no better advocates than the signatories to the 1916 Easter Proclamation, of republicans and socialists, who fought and died for a destiny to which they felt called. Patrick Pearse read out the proclamation, usually attributed to him, with some assistance from the Marxist socialist James Connolly, outside the General Post Office in Dublin. In his final sentence he called for sacrifice "for the common good". We are fortunate that in our modern age we can claim rights for the common good peaceably, and reflect that society is rarely served by change through force of arms. Nevertheless, we can be as animated and dedicated as our forebears in our claim for justice, equity, and fairness.

A party's identity is seen as crucial in determining connection and electoral relevance. Identity is part of something far deeper however, and that is ego. Our ego, our complete body and soul, self-image and being that encompasses how we think, feel, and use our will to distinguish who we are, separates and identifies us from others. It is reflected in personality and character. Ego often determines relationship. As an individual I may consider myself a nice person, thoughtful and fun, others may not, but those who decide whether to befriend me or not, will not list my virtues before inviting me for a get-together, they will instinctively consider me authentic or not, someone they like or not, someone who could be a friend or not, to be trusted or not. True self will normally be discovered by those who know us, it just takes time. I know my understanding of self is not always shared by even those closest to me. A political party, like any corporate body, will have its own establishment ego.

Values and virtues may inform identity, political identity may present character and beliefs, but it is ego that determines the long-term relationship with the electorate. Parties that are confused about their identity, display a fragmented ego, or fail to acknowledge its importance in determining who they are will struggle to be considered authentic, trustworthy, and credible, irrespective of the values they hold, or the identity they present. Red roses or red flags, commendable virtues and values, objects of identity must be an expression of true self, of ego, to resonate meaningfully with the public. The Labour Party struggles to identify ego and self, the Liberal Democrats, perhaps reflecting individual member's attitudes, denies ego. It comes as little surprise that authenticity was attached to the former Conservative Prime Minister, Boris Johnson, a man exuding an appreciation and awareness of self and ego to good electoral effect in 2019.

A paradigm shift towards a societal philosophy may come more easily to the Labour Party; a party founded to pursue collectivist claims over the economy. On the other hand, the ideological trauma the Labour Party has suffered in recent decades, over the nature and relevance of socialism and its foundational status, may make it difficult for Party and membership to countenance another ideology, even one that can co-exist with their existing values, irrespective of the benefits that may accrue from it, for Party and the people the Party aims to represent.

For the Liberal Democrats the philosophy of society accords closely with its stated values, remarkably so, but their aspirations for the individual have not been allied to a collectivist philosophy, so what might at first glance appear a natural process of evolution, explicitly leaning towards a societal framework for economy and policy development, may be too much for the Party and its members to endorse.

There is of course a third option, the unforeseeable future in which neither of the two main, primarily English, opposition parties evolve significantly, and a new party or group emerge to fill the vacuum which exists in the radicalised, extended, centre ground of politics, a Society Party.

The Green Party

The Green Party is powerfully persuasive beyond its electoral voice. Its message of environmentalism is now mainstream, the argument has been won over the need for sustainable, responsible economic development, as has the case for moving the dynamic of the economy away from carbon, towards cleaner and sustainable energy solutions to combat the effect of global warming as climate changes. The Green Party, and its membership, keeps a watchful eye on the activities of those who are environmentally irresponsible. Many people who may not vote for them will share their views on the environment. The Party advocates a steady-state economy with regulated capitalism, a softer position than that adopted by the Green Party of the US, who in 2016 passed a motion in favour of rejecting both capitalism and state socialism, supporting instead an "alternative economic system based on ecology and decentralisation of power".[49] The roots of Green Party economic policy, influenced through the energy and diversity of its membership, however, in many respects lay beyond the scope of traditional market economics, perhaps making systemic economic reform through a societal sector unimaginable. The politics of an alternative economy, delivering the common cause of an environmental agenda, may not sit easily with acceptance of a reformed market economy as a driver for change.

Eight of the ten Green Party's core values which guide their "new and radical kind of politics", connect directly to the foundational attributes of a societal economy. In the first of these core values, the Green Party "understand that the threats to economic, social and environmental well-being are part of the same problem and recognise that solving one of these crises cannot be achieved without solving the others". This recognises the important, interdependent causal loop which determines well-being, between economy, society and "human fulfilment". A desire to grow personal wealth beyond reason, the unfettered capitalist system which enabled this to happen, harmed the environment and threatens life on our planet, the interconnectedness is clear. The Philosophical Basis of the Green Party links a vision for humanity, democracy, freedom, progress, and society together in a meaningful restatement of systemic values. It lays out an economic programme which highlights how one can reformulate the existing economic system to achieve its aims, including the development of a 'third sector'.

The Green Party then, once more, is pushing the boundaries towards paradigm change, and environmentalism in its broader sense, of our societal environment, not just our physical one. The physical and natural world, the economy and society have overlapping ecosystems and their relationship to one another determines well-being and lived experience.

Ask the general population, what do the Green Party stand for, and I suspect most people will say, "protecting the environment". Ask, what alternative economy does the Green Party believe in and I imagine the reply will be "a green economy", "a fairer one, a sustainable one".

Kate Raworth's doughnut economics gives a framework for sustainable development, visualising the safe and just space which humanity can inhabit in a regenerative and distributive economy, with its boundaries set by an ecological ceiling, and a social foundation where life's essentials are met. It has been described as a compass guiding human progress. The Green Party economy, one which speaks to its values, and challenges the current paradigm, draws on Kate Raworth's work. It cannot be realised through capitalism. The circular economy, like circular concepts, is confronted by the power of linear relationships, based on hierarchy, wealth, and ownership.

A societist programme and ideology is entirely consistent with green politics. Indeed, they are intertwined. Environmentalism addresses impacts we all experience. Collective rights, driven by our collective will, have been asserted, forcing compliance with environmentally aware policy. It is precisely this power to change, which political and economic reformation through societism seeks to achieve.

Scottish and Welsh nationalism and independence

I can only offer impressions, vague notions of how an ideology asserting societal rights would apply independently in Scotland and Wales.

Principles promoting the collective common good, and associated individual rights, are universal and global. Societal rights linked to the global market economy, can exist whether a nation is governed by authoritarian control or oligarchical influence. Markets and the enterprises which serve them generally operate beyond the hand of government. However, our concept of freedom, informed as it is by an appreciation and expectation of democratic governance, suggests this may be more difficult, or impossible, in undemocratic societies.

Pan European ideals underpin the development of the EU, yet each nation retains its national sovereignty, attaching to the uniqueness of their societies. It is important to recognise that each nation and its society has different societal values, and expresses its will in different ways, even though we share many of our core, human, universal values. The same applies to the nations of the UK.

Scottish and Welsh societies are identifiably different from England, nations that had similar experiences to

England, but whose societal values and identity are subtly, but in other ways clearly, undeniably different.

The founder of the Labour Party and its first parliamentary leader, chosen in 1906, was Keir Hardie, born in the central Lowlands of Scotland, he worked in the mines of Lanarkshire from the age of ten, led the Ayrshire Miners' Union, and was a member of parliament for Merthyr Tydfil in South Wales. He thought at heart that the Celtic people were all communists, giving a flavour of the society he inhabited, although this is likely to be based on an interpretation of Welsh Society dating back to the Middle Ages, including the importance of equality and fair distribution of property which can be traced back to a system of land distribution that was not based on the Norman concept of primogeniture, under which property was inherited by the oldest son.[50] The cause of workers representation, and the class politics of socialism, forged in the valleys of South Wales and the shipyards and slums of Glasgow, responded to, and reflected societal characteristics of the two nations distinct from England.

As an outsider I cannot begin to understand how the societal inheritance from the tribal and clan systems of Scotland, overlaid by the Acts of Union, described by Simon Schama as a "hostile merger", may have affected current values and societal perspective but it will have done so.[51] The use of force to achieve acquiescence between England and the other nations of the UK has long since given way to a parliamentary settlement, but that history of union, government from Westminster, and the sense of subordination that centralised rule, monarchical in origin, imbues in diverse ways affects society today.

It is no co-incidence following Labour's electoral decline in Scotland, de-industrialisation and diminishing social class identification, that collectivist societal expression, is to be found in a call for Scottish national independence.

It may be that Scotland and Wales, because of their history and culture, will be a fertile ground for the growth of societism. Indeed, the SNP declaring themselves a party and currently one of Government which is centre left, pursue the politics of identity, of national identity. For this reason, they are a party who frame much of their policy according to societal instinct and the public good, a party that is, in many respects societist but governing without an economic system that attaches to that system of governance. It can be argued that attributes of societism drive Scotland towards independence, an appreciation of the politics of the common good, rooted in a unique and identifiable societal separateness from the rest of the UK.

It is the disjuncture between societal difference and nation statehood which often results in conflict, including some of the hardest to resolve peaceably. This is the case in Ireland, where societal difference, identified through religious affiliation, entrenched by opposing allegiance to two nation states on one island, has resulted in conflict and loss of life for centuries. Societal identification with Europe helped communities in conflict to value their commonality, rather than accept their segregation by difference, during the peace process. It is little wonder that underlying tensions have arisen post-Brexit. If we look behind statehood to society, expound principles for the good of community rather than state, then the process of peaceful resolve and co-existence may be helped.

In contrast to the Scottish Nationalist Party, Plaid Cymru remains a nationalist and democratic socialist party. However, it too is largely societist. If one scrutinises the party's eleven key policies in their 2019 General Election manifesto, they are not socialist but societist. There is no mention, nor appeal to the politics of ownership of the means of production or distribution on behalf of the Welsh people. Instead, the party proposes a selection of social policy and spending priorities for the common good, which attach to their vision of what Welsh society is, and how it should function: backing a second EU referendum, a vision of Welsh society operating within a pan-European framework, spending on 'green jobs', electrification of the main rail lines, providing free social care, drugs law reform, income support for low-income families, education spending, opposition to new nuclear sites, police officer recruitment, devolution of tax powers, and a call for devolved parliaments to be able to decide whether the nation should go to war. These are not necessarily socialist policies, they are all societist.

The societal, 'centre' ground of politics

Benjamin Franklin, in 1789, famously quoted the idiom that there are two certainties, death and taxes. The quantum of tax is less certain. There is one certainty I would add, that we live inescapably on a human and natural spectrum, centring on the average. It is a mathematical truth.

The spectrum of profit a societal sector occupies, stretches from non-profit social enterprise at one extreme of the spectrum, through to the point where shareholder interest determines purpose and outcome at the other. This accords closely to the political spectrum which we call the centre but is in fact far larger.

Conservatism attaches the extreme end of the economic spectrum, where shareholder interest determines purpose and outcome, to the electorate, in the belief that private sector self-interest achieves the best outcomes for the general population too. Because there is no universal model attaching any sector, other than the private sector, to the market economy, Conservatism pulls the political centre towards its extreme position on the economic spectrum. This positioning, the product of legacy, and entitlement attached to pre-existing wealth is made possible because the general population do not have the primary rights over the economy they should. Our political idea of the centre ground is distorted by this causal link between how the market economy currently functions and the political framework it produces.

The societal centre ground of politics, which is not just central but tends towards the average, stretches across a landscape we identify currently as being occupied by the radical left through to the liberal right. Individuals will always see different and competing systems and programmes as more or less relevant to their personal values. This justifies parties with similar aims existing independently of one another, motivated by different but overlapping core values.

However, those deeming Society to be a distinct political entity, connecting the electorate directly to the market economy through a societal sector, will have a unique vision of how a societal political and economic framework can improve lives, and the means to do so.

The last time this happened in the UK was when the Fabians, in alliance with the Trades Union movement gave birth to the Labour Party. Following the marginalisation, then obscurity of socialism, based on production control, as a real economic force, what economic system fills the void for those opposing monopoly capitalism if not market societism?

* * *

The power of a government, connecting national interest with the economy is one that can transform outcomes. Governments, often from less democratic countries, have recognised this in the hybrid forms of capitalism that they adapt, connecting state to economy. Russia and China offer alternative models of statist capitalism, as do countries growing sovereign wealth funds, succeeding in growing capitalist economies which serve their national self-interest. This has led those in the liberal democracies, to conflate the issue of a democratic deficit with a crisis in capitalism. The democratic deficit arises because there is no unity of purpose around shared economic objectives, not because capitalism is in crisis, it regularly manifests crises, but because in its exclusivity it cannot meet our national and societal needs and never will. Exclusive reliance on capitalism and the private sector in the market economy is the cause of the democratic deficit, not its solution.

Representative democracy is strong when it serves society's best interests. Weakness lays, not in democracy's inherent attributes, but through its association with capitalism and the intrinsic failings of that economic model, driven as it is primarily by personal self-interest. Liberal democracy is constructed on the foundation stone of individual social and electoral rights. The paradox is that individualism, finding a counterpart in the individualism of capitalism, becomes frail when capitalism erodes the bonds that unify society. Societism's greatest contribution may be to strengthen our democracy, by establishing collective bonds around unified economic purpose. The combination of democracy and capitalism can lead to weakness, the symbiosis of democratic values and societism will lead to stronger democracy.

There are universal political, economic, and human rights which attach to the individual. These are not based on whether a person lives in a democracy or not, they are indeed universal, and personal, and they exist beyond national boundaries. The global market-economy operating beyond borders should embed these rights. A general population denied societal human and economic rights is vulnerable to the imposition of outcomes by those with power. This is true in the matter of economics, just as it is in that of war or other human crises, where governments override the best interest of the populations they represent or of those whose governments they wish to challenge. It is often said that power demands respect. If this is so, then it is hardly surprising and wholly unacceptable that the global, general population are denied economic rights giving them power, which governments may choose to ignore, including a right to be respected.

Politicians, of the centre and left, and the fellowship of reformers seeking greater fairness and economic justice, need to breathe in the air of change and power that comes to them through a societal economy working for the common good, through an economy that operates to their values and of those they seek to represent, a call for re-engagement, representation, and responsibility through systemic reform.

Chapter 5

SOCIETISATION and MARKET SOCIETISM – Economic Justice and Opportunity

This land is your land, this land is my land
This land was made for you and me

Woody Guthrie, This Land is Your Land[52]

For over two hundred years, from a time when the furnaces and mills of Victorian Britain heralded the arrival of industrial revolution, and capitalism, to the modern day, the foundational elements of our economy, of market economics, its ethical contradictions, and the way it operates has changed little, despite huge societal change. There are two fundamental questions. First, who owns the economy and for whose benefit does it operate? Second, if not, or if not only, capitalism, what?

There is also a why? and a how? Why have we not seen any systemic alternative to capitalism evolve? Capitalism is ascendant across the globe. Even once ardent communist and socialist governments, who advocated state ownership and central planning, now embrace the economics of capitalism, and accept the reality that our world functions through competition, and free, open markets.

How does a person, who is not a business owner, enjoy the maximum benefits the economy can offer through the democracy of consumerism, and free choice in a market economy? Economic democratisation can exist where markets exist, beyond the hand of government. The private sector conveys rights associated with individual exceptionalism and ownership. The purpose of a societal sector is to increase the economic rights of the general population based on our commonality. Commonality is distinct from collectivist claims generally linked to production ownership. Collectivism is defined by group representation, where commonality derives from our natural and universal, human state of being.

We are, collectively, naturally average, an average state we share on the broad curve at the top of the bell jar. We can neither deny nor escape this definition. We are spectrum, all exhibiting an array of abilities, talents, and traits which others share to a greater or lesser degree. It is this similarity, of ability, aptitude and outlook that helps us live together, an essential balance arising from the limitations of our existence, constrained by our physical bodies, brain power and lifespan. It explains why we can cohabit in society, without difference tearing us apart.

It is wonderful that exceptional qualities, of commercial acumen and endeavour, lead to positive financial outcomes for many individuals. Nevertheless, our economy should be designed to intrinsically promote the best possible outcomes for the broad base of our population too, the greater number of the average, identified as of society. It should also serve those at one end of the spectrum, who are particularly vulnerable, disempowered or relatively poor, when private sector exceptionalism lays at the polar, furthest end of the spectrum from them.

Averageness is a universal value, as are random fluctuations from the average. It can be observed around us in the turning of the seasons, our climate, and of life itself, in our age and health, the spectrum of colour we are able to see, and sound we can hear. Yet, we facilitate advantage, and rights attaching to advancement through measures of meritocratic exceptionalism, and individual opportunity. Merit deserves reward, but what is merited, and which human and societal values does it attach to, academic success, entrepreneurial ambition, or selfless giving to others? Limiting notions of meritocracy can reduce our appreciation of the average state of humanity, and the rights that the greater number of us should enjoy not because we are exceptional, we all are given the random circumstance of birth, but because we are not.

The forces which tend the natural world towards the average also move nature towards equilibrium. After a short summer storm, I was walking at the foot of the South Downs, wandering through some quiet lanes. Mist was rising from the fields, like an early morning dew, and droplets fell from the trees as temperature fell and the heat of the day gave way to a fresher, cooler evening. The powerful force of the storm returned the local environment to its normal, average summer temperature.

Of global significance, our planet's equilibrium has been disturbed. An environment on Earth that evolved over many millions of years, inexorably seeks now, through extreme reactions and events to find a new equilibrium, a balance of temperature, weather, and habitat for life. Our economy disturbs this global, natural equilibrium. There is a further relationship of equilibrium, that between our human nature and economy. There is an equilibrium between well-being, our experience of life, and the economic system. A societal economy searches for a healthy and sustainable equilibrium between economy and society, humanity, and the planet.

Capitalism adheres advantage to individual exceptionalism and survives, largely conceptually unchallenged for many reasons touched on throughout earlier chapters. Power, self-interest, unrepresentative governance, unconscious acceptance, fear, deeply ingrained inherited ideas, all contribute to stasis, a failure to adapt as society evolves. If a person can struggle to develop, and becomes set in their ways, reaches maturity, and does not challenge self then how much harder for us to do so collectively.

Societisation can only be achieved therefore where there is means and motivation, where we can identify ways of reshaping the economy towards common good outcomes, and there is a will, political and intellectual to make it happen.

A central aim of a societal sector is to increase competition in free-markets, reducing imperfections in the way they function, elevating consumer rights to improve the standard of living and well-being of the general population, through access to the surpluses free-markets generate, and through lower prices for goods and services.

Societisation goes beyond the issue of competitive enterprise. Once one acknowledges the rights that attach to the economy, of the individual as a member of society, and of the collective that is society, and give it the attributes of a separate, unique, and identifiable entity then our conception of policy and economic management changes.

Societal economics is founded on:

- Elevating societal purpose through perpetual, societally purposed trusts, and companies.
- Recognising collective, societal rights over the profits free and open markets generate, by using profit to impact social need, and fund social expenditure, or reducing it to offer consumers a better deal, or to benefit other stakeholders.
- Increasing competitiveness through the development of a societal sector, ending the systemic monopoly private sector capitalism enjoys over the free market economy.
- Establishing a pool of capital to finance a societal sector.
- Reconsidering the power, nature and obligations arising from public borrowing, public spending, and the role of state.
- Rebalancing risk and reward in the economy. Acknowledging reciprocity, of the contribution we

collectively, as a society, make towards the economy, and the commensurate rights and benefits that should flow from that.

- Redefining what profit is and how that determines well-being. Profit in a societal sector, like the economy it fosters, need only be sustainable and sufficient. Enterprises need only generate sufficient profit to fund their societal purpose and sustain their business model. A societal appreciation of profit is measured by the good it can achieve, not just the wealth it can create.

- Inverting the values and goals attributable to the private sector, of personal gain and self, in favour of well-being, and social purpose for the collective good.

Corporate form and the social, third and fourth sectors

Search government advice on setting up a company and two primary options are offered. The first, a company limited by shares, which is legally separate from the people who own and run it, has separate finances from the personal ones of its owners, has shares and shareholders, and are "usually businesses that make a profit".

There is an alternative, the company limited by guarantee, usually "not for profit". It too has a separate legal identity with its finances separated from the personal ones of its owners. It does not have shareholders, but guarantors and a 'guaranteed amount', and invests profits it makes back into the company. It can distribute its profits but then would not be eligible for charitable status.

The bridge between companies formed by shareholders for profit and guarantee companies, formed generally for non-profit purpose, is provided by the Community Interest Company ("CIC"). The CIC is designed for social enterprise and is structured like a normal limited company, either limited by shares or guarantee, but is driven by the community purpose set out in its constitution, has an asset lock to make sure assets are used to benefit the community, with a cap on the profits which can be distributed as dividends that cannot exceed 35%.

We have corporate forms, the company limited by guarantee, and CICs which are likely to appeal to founders pursuing a social purpose who could compete in the market economy against shareholder owned companies, yet systemically, at scale, they have failed to do so.

The company limited by guarantee, identified through a non-profit purpose, is often formed as a charity with a favourable tax status. As soon as a company is one distributing profit to its guarantors, thereby being ineligible for charitable status, founders are encouraged to set their business up as one owned by shareholders. The guarantee company does not exist to compete, through a ubiquitous and homogenous form, against shareholder companies, rather to offer an alternative structure, generally for non-profit goals.

There are companies which are formed by guarantee and are profit-driven, investing their profits in the business rather than distributing it to shareholders. BUPA, the health insurance, and healthcare group is one such example. It is an anomaly, the clue to its origins is to be found in its original name, the British United Provident Association. Provident associations were legal entities for trading, or for voluntary organisation, with a historical antecedence in the mutual and friendly societies founded in the Victorian age, often by wealthy patrons to help those less fortunate, by establishing businesses operating for the benefit of the community. They operated for members interests, through mutual or community purpose, businesses recognising the benefits arising from interdependence, and the strength of collective consumerism. BUPA is a member-oriented organisation, commonly considered to be a private health company for the very reason that it is not societal, and therefore, not defined by its non-profit purpose but rather members' interests.

The CIC exists in part to bridge this gap, between for-profit activity and social purpose, entrepreneurial ambition, and well-being outcomes. There were 5.1 million companies registered at Companies House in March 2023, with 801,000 formations during the year. By contrast in the preceding year there were only 26,000 registered CICs, with 5,339 having been registered in the year ending March 2022. This compares with four types of legally constituted charities, around 100,000 unincorporated charities and community Benefit Societies. On formation the Office of the Regulator of Community Interest Companies decides whether an organisation is eligible to become a CIC and whether it passes a community interest test. An organisation's activities must benefit the community, which can include the use of its profit for charitable or other community benefit purposes. Generally, purpose is directed towards localised geographical or group needs, part of a societal framework, but an incomplete one. One measure of the relative insignificance of the CIC, despite its reformist potential, is that the Regulator of CICs works part-time and is supported by only seven members of staff.

If I wish to set up a private company, there is no ethical criteria which prevent me from doing so, within a day. It is sufficient that I decide to collaborate with other shareholders to undertake activities generating distributable profit. In the social, third and fourth sectors, the CIC must receive an ethical stamp of approval on formation and its ongoing status depends on adhering to its non-profit purpose and having limitations on the element of profit which is distributed. This is in many respects useful and provides a legal, corporate framework for the development of a societal sector. However, private sector corporate formation allows shareholders to fast-track incorporation, by self-identifying themselves as capitalists interested in combining for profit, whereas those combining to form a societal entity for a 'communal cause' cannot do so. This is a double whammy because every CIC must be registered at Companies House, just like any standard limited company, but there is further paperwork and an approval process that might put off people from starting potential CICs.

The advantages of forming a company as a CIC are limited. It is a corporate form which clearly identifies the organisation as societally purposed. It also opens the possibility of attracting finance available only to charities and community interest companies. However, there are no tax breaks and unlike charities it pays tax like any private sector business. The CIC is part of a diverse and complex range of options for business structures operating beyond private sector objectives, but diversity is both a strength and a potentially fatal weakness.

The definition of a company as societal at its conception should be as straightforward as labelling one as "private", as accessible during the formation process as the simplicity of a click on a formation website, which is currently available for private but not social interest companies. A legal framework can then develop around the ubiquity of this corporate form, just as it has done for governance of the private sector. The existing legal framework functions with limited scope because we conceive the economy in a diminished form, a manifestation of the legacy impact discussed throughout this book. This also finds expression in the related uncertainty, diversity, and definition of the "third, fourth" and "social" sectors.

The third sector includes charities, social enterprises, and voluntary groups. The social sector appears imprecise but comprises development and welfare activities provided by non-government agencies and government. Undoubtedly these form part of a broad societal framework, of organisations created to achieve purposes benefitting society, in the main through non-profit, not-for-profit, philanthropic, and mission-based activities. The antecedence of these sectors, all serving societal best interest, lays in the philanthropic, charitable, and mutual interest organisations established to reduce socially unacceptable outcomes. This is a benevolent response to need rather than a demand that need be met through economic rights.

The fourth sector moves towards a defined societal sector, one that combines the market-based approaches of the private sector with the social and environmental aims of the public and non-profit sectors. The Fourth Sector group, supporting the development of a fourth sector, recognise that despite the massive growth and contributions of the sector "we have not been able to advance the system far enough, fast enough. The lack of coordination between these efforts, combined with the boundaries and constraints imposed by the current dominant systems, limit the degree of progress any intervention has been able to make". Reference to the dominant system concerns the limitations imposed by existing paradigm frameworks. Interventions can achieve well-being outcomes but will only advance at scale when connected to a political will born of rights.

The absence of a political will to develop a system which can radically change outcomes is born of a mixture of confusion and a belief in the current framework, that the best ways forward have already been identified.

Labour in its set of five missions around which they will build a manifesto, link outcomes making sure people are "better off" to "the opportunities they need to succeed", "breaking down the barriers to opportunity". Whilst worthwhile, it makes the causal link between personal attainment through opportunity, not the immediacy of reform changing how the economy delivers fairer outcomes in the first place. Their mission relies on "government departments working together, business working with unions, the private sector working with the public sector, and a common partnership between national and local government". This is a familiar framework which does not embrace the development of a societal, fourth sector, nor a socialist economy rooted in its past, instead relying on the private and public sectors, managed through State intervention. It does not conceive of economic reform.

The Liberal Democratic Party aspires to a values driven society concerned with well-being outcomes, but the means are less clear. The overarching plan for the economy, is to achieve increasing investment, prosperity, and fairness by making taxes fair and ensuring spending does not exceed the money raised in taxes over the medium term, "with additional flexibility during periods of economic crisis". There is no connection between economic reform and the aspirations they seek. They face a catch-22, that fairness depends on meeting social need and if taxes are insufficient it is impossible to balance the books, so that social need goes unmet or has to be funded by debt, placing an unfair burden on future generations.

The Green Party places its policy EC620, under the heading the 'third sector'. In that policy it states that "special attention will be paid to the third sector of the economy, which combines the discipline and flexibility of the private sector, the accountability and the community-responsiveness of the public sector, the social concern of the voluntary sector and the activities of the informal economy". It recognises that an alternative sector exists but in the absence of definition, describes it by reference to features exhibited by other sectors.

The position of all the current parties, opposing the dominance of shareholder interest in the economy, betray their reliance on that interest by failing to name and claim any alternative to it. This legacy thinking condemns us to search within the current framework for solutions to economic and social problems when history teaches us there are no solutions within the current system. It is both cause and consequence, that the framework for the formation of companies, limitations in corporate form and legal scope, has its counterpart, the lack of definition of the social, third and fourth sectors of the economy, evidenced by the absence of any meaningful recognition of their role in fundamentally reforming the economy.

It is hardly surprising that a sector which does not explicitly define itself by name, choosing to do so by reference to the existing framework will struggle to connect to a political constituency which will seek change around its attributes. The fourth sector is ill defined. If neither private nor public, what is it, if not societal, and if it is a societal sector differentiated by unique characteristics then it needs to empower itself by acknowledging that it connects to a political will through the outcomes those features of their sector can deliver. This concerns not just the sector but the social funding which supports that sector.

Social funding, perhaps like our notion of the third, social, and to a lesser extent, the fourth sector, has its antecedence in the philanthropy of those who support well-being outcomes in society. The work of the philanthropically informed sectors is critical in securing economic and social outcomes which would otherwise be denied the general population, often affecting those most marginalised in society and in need. It will always be required. However, it is rooted in patronage not rights, pleas not demands, legacy economics not a practical ambition to change the inherent workings of the economy. The philanthropic sectors should be complemented by their counterpart, a fully developed societal sector demanding collective rights over the market economy, supported by a fully developed commercial social funding community, including governments committed to policies of societal best interest.

It remains that unlike the shareholder owned company, which is capitalist and symbiotically attached to the ideology of capitalism and Conservatism, there is no corporate form which adheres the best, well-being interest of the general population inherently and intrinsically to the market economy. There is no philosophy or political commitment which supports the development of such an economy and without it there is no reason to suppose progress will not be perpetually limited.

There is no body of political philosophy associated with any company form which is supported and adheres through modern doctrine and belief to any political party, other than capitalism to the Conservative Party through shareholder ownership. The issue of social reform, the significance of the philanthropic and social funding communities and of meaningful reform is a political issue and cannot be avoided.

Two organisations in the UK, Greenwich Leisure Ltd, GLL, operating under the Better Gym brand name and the BBC, deserve consideration because they are, in different ways, societal. One a trading enterprise, the other a public service broadcaster, both competing against shareholder owned companies in the free market, operating beyond the horizon of maximising shareholder wealth.

We can be inspired by two overseas companies. Motkraft in Norway, and Yvonne Chouinard's Patagonia Group. Motkraft generates profit, purposed to reduce energy costs for households.

"Truth be told, there were no good options available, so we created our own", said Yvonne Chouinard, as he moved Patagonia to, "going purpose". Patagonia is a certified B corp, a for-profit company, with a trust company structure established to generate impactful profits through purpose. Patagonia and Motkraft, signpost the way for the development of a societal sector. Patagonia advances with the wisdom of age, Motkraft through the galvanising energy of its young founders.

Gyms, leisure facilities, and libraries are provided by GLL, a basket of core services arising naturally, from its establishment in 1993 to run local services in the London Borough of Greenwich. This it does as a non-profit distributing co-operative, running services on behalf of local authorities across the UK. The company is a social enterprise, structured as an Industrial and Provident Society for the benefit of the community, with its co-operative members and therefore owners, comprising the company's workers, managed by a trust board of elected members of staff, and representatives of other stakeholders, including Greenwich Council. It characterises its core activity as socially purposeful and is registered as a non-profit charity under the Co-operative and Community Benefit Societies Act 2014. Like BUPA, but for different reasons, GLL is anomalous, competitive in the free market, defined as a charity, a non-profit enterprise but one making a profit. Its charitable status exempts it from UK tax. Its corporate form and definition as a non-profit charity, mean this form of enterprise cannot be systemically integrated into the market economy.

The current compromise offered society is that social purpose in the market economy is to be achieved by annexing non-profit goals to shareholder owned companies, through a 'moral compass', and shareholder virtues of social responsibility. This pursuit of corporate, non-profit purpose is commendable, but reduces the ambition we have for systemic economic reform able to answer the question, "if not capitalism, what"?

One cannot rely on member owned enterprises to deliver social purpose, whether shareholder-owned, or by other members. Shareholder and member interest, linked to property rights, is defined by the members control, unlike perpetual, purpose trust companies which are defined by their purpose. In July 2023, Home Reit, a specialist in housing for the homeless, decided to drop its social purpose investment policy. The board, seeking shareholder approval, aim to give itself free rein to invest in any residential property it chooses and "re-tenant" the portfolio "to maximise income and capital returns".

The BBC is partly commercial, with around a quarter of its revenue coming from commercial activities and is funded by the public through its licence fee, accountable to government, operating under its Agreement with the Secretary of State for Digital, Culture, Media, and Sport. The BBC is the UK's national, public service broadcaster. We may agree or disagree with certain of its actions, but it is a constant presence throughout many people's lives. It aims to reflect our diversity, being informative, entertaining, of a presence that can be reassuring, yet at times also infuriating. It is in essence societal.

The BBC's mission is "to act in the public interest, serving all audiences through the provision of impartial, high-quality and distinctive output and services which inform, educate and entertain". There are five public purposes related to programming and its role reflecting societal values and diversity. The BBC exemplifies enterprise, outside the charitable, community sector, that is not shareholder owned, which is successful and societal. It is little wonder that it is an anathema to many who advocate the exclusive primacy of the shareholder owned company.

GLL and the BBC are each restricted, one by its charitable, not-for profit status, the other through its charter and governmental oversight, from the freedom to act unencumbered in the free market. Both corporations are societal, but in form not ubiquitously so. They are both anomalies.

Governance, management, and accountability structures for enterprises which are not shareholder owned, like those which are, can be prescribed at birth through their statutory formation documents. The operational responsibilities of a Board of Trustees are identical to a Board of Directors but directed to its purposes defined beyond profit. Societal purpose makes companies directly responsible to a wider range of stakeholders, including the court of public opinion. It is inevitable and appropriate that a societal endeavour will, and should, be held to high standards of acceptable behaviour. It is one feature of societal reform, to assert values that transcend personal gain, and self-centred action.

Competition and Free Markets – societal rights over free-market profits

Free markets are the tracks along which our competitive, enterprise economy run. They are neither inherently good, nor bad. What determines their function is the type of business which serves them, the values, and ethics of those who operate those businesses, and the purposes for which those businesses operate.

They are, at their basic level, simply markets where consumers are served by producers, both exercising their free-will, one choosing to purchase, and the other to supply goods and services, from and to that market, with price determined by the forces of supply and demand.

The right to profit vests in producers, by virtue of shareholders' control and property ownership of assets. Consumers, on the other hand, constitute a largely atomised group of individuals. However, it is only corporate form which denies consumers rights over the profits their purchasing power generates, and as stakeholders, their interest in the enterprises which serve them.

Motkraft, in Norway, was started by a group of students from the Norwegian University of Science and Technology. Their purpose is to "fight for electricity customers, not against them", by keeping prices down, to give the cheapest and safest deals, as a self-declared "Resistance" on the side of their customers. They list the defects in the energy market, characterised by tempting offers, unannounced price increases, high termination fees and aggressive telephone sales. They are clear, they started precisely in protest to this market abuse, so that their customers will pay less. They are passionate and purposeful. The business model is to generate sufficient profit from their sales to sustain the company's operation, paid for by a fee covering their running costs, so that they do not need to make a big profit from consumption. They do this by charging for energy use at cost, at the spot price, and charging a small surcharge and a minimum monthly fee, to cover the costs of operating Motkraft. The cost to business customers is also kept low. The company employs staff "passionately and purposefully" committed to its work. The business purpose is linked to wider aims of a better, sustainable future.

What type of company is Motkraft? It generates a profit from the sale of electricity, so it is clearly for-profit, neither a charity nor a not-for-profit enterprise. It is a social enterprise, defined by its non-profit purpose, but also defined by its for-profit purpose, delivering low-cost electricity for its customers. The label 'not-for-profit' social enterprise, in its generality, diminishes its status, and relevance to the market economy.

In our most basic formulation of economics, embodying private sector values, producers seek to maximise profits for owners. Motkraft defy this outcome by seeking to earn sufficient profit to sustainably operate their business. For Motkraft profit is spectrum, defined not by supply and demand and wealth creation, but by purpose. Further, where the private sector separates consumer and producer interest, represented by two separate curves on a demand and supply graph, Motkraft unify them.

This unification of producer purpose and virtue-driven consumerism is of paramount significance. The separation of producer and consumer interest produces a society which itself is atomised and fractured by competing claims for resource. In the Motkraft enterprise, personal and collective self-interest converge through its corporate purpose. Society is unified around shared purpose and common outcomes. Motkraft is a societal company. It should be placed within the working framework of a societal sector, with all the resource which should be developed around that sector.

Private sector form takes primacy over democratic economic and societal rights, with power becoming exercisable by those with pre-existing wealth, according to the size of that wealth. It is inherently undemocratic. Motkraft, democratise the economy, by giving consumers choice, to buy from them, supporting their societal purpose, or another company building shareholder wealth. Virtue-driven consumers, purchasing from companies whose purposes they believe in, have power.

This democratising power can determine which companies are successful, how resources are allocated, and ultimately the share of national wealth which is privatised or societised. Every pound of distributable profit generated in a societal sector, above the general level of taxation, becomes a pound less that the state may need to borrow to meet a collective or social need.

Motkraft offers more competitive outcomes, perfecting the failure of the private sector to deliver the very thing we are told it is best at, delivering competitive prices. Shareholder purpose prevents this in the case of energy. Rather than having plural corporate forms, including a societal sector, which increases sectoral competition and lowers the cost of living, we allow a private sectoral monopoly to endure, and when it fails, attempt to rectify it through governance and regulation.

The Competition and Markets Authority exists to promote competition for the benefit of consumers, a tacit admission that the private sector cannot inherently deliver the freely competitive outcomes we are taught it should. In its 2020 report, State of UK Competition, the Authority noted that competition across the economy had declined over the last twenty years, with concentration of supply in fewer operators rising, causing mark-ups to be increased. It is therefore evolving a new unit to deal with the monopolising forces of the digital economy. Consumers pay more, but lower paid workers suffer twice over, through uncompetitive market forces and profit maximisation, as consumers through higher prices, and as employees when wages are depressed. It has been estimated that 32.5 million people, 60% of the adult population are also workers.[53] The work of this Authority is another feature of the private sector economy, reliance on regulation and governance to deal with its inherent defects.

We are so conditioned to accept that free-market profits are privately owned, that we allow private equity to assert claims over future profits and productivity, without asking the obvious question: what of public rights unrelated to share 'equity'?

Language is important, private equity, or publicly quoted equity, may be equitable between the rights afforded a group of shareholders, but there is nothing equitable, or just about how property rights, linked to pre-existing capital, diminish the rights of the general population to share directly in our national wealth.

All equity is private, just some more private than other. 'Private equity' commonly refers to private equity which is not publicly quoted. It seeks the purer privatisation of profit that we observed when early joint venture, and colonisation, took place, to acquire resources and profits for the benefit of the fewest number with privileged access to a venture.

The extraction of profit from our national wealth, redirected towards the accumulation of privatised wealth beyond reason, is indefensible, particularly when it is made possible by monopoly rights over the market economy. Shareholder equity seeks privatisation of the profit markets generate and passes the costs of social cohesion onto society. We all pay higher taxes and indebt future generations because of it.

Like all privately owned business, private equity owned companies and partnerships make good and bad choices which affects the lives of all the stakeholders in the companies they target, including employees, consumers, and wider society. This is as it is. The existence of private equity firms is neither necessarily good nor bad, but inevitable in an economy dominated by private ownership. In a world where the ordinary person in the street can theoretically become a shareholder by purchasing shares on publicly quoted exchanges, it is natural for some shareholders to band together, through exclusive forms of ownership, to maximise their private gains.

Private equity's net asset value has grown more than sevenfold since 2002, and in the US the number of private equity backed companies more than doubled between 2006 and 2017, meanwhile publicly traded firms fell by

16%.[54] The Treasury has examined private equity deals, as concern grows over the pace and number of takeovers of British companies. Aggressive acquisition is directed towards maximising profit and shareholder benefit, not societal and consumer good. Food, housing, heat and light, water and a multitude of other services and goods are necessities of life, their provision determining our well-being. A consumer should have choice, whether to be served by a societal company working for their good, or a private equity influenced one engineered to maximise returns for shareholders, and by so doing, reducing their well-being.

Privatisation is not necessarily bad; it can lead to productive growth. However, from a societal viewpoint it is wrong that the economy can be privatised in this way. An economy already dominated by privately owned enterprise, is being increasingly owned by companies in which the public cannot buy shares. Further, there must be equanimity within our economy, the balance that comes from having private equity at one end of our spectrum of enterprise, and another form of enterprise serving the rest of the spectrum, securing public, collective rights over future profit.

A societal economy must be credible, practicable and achieve its aims. We must therefore consider whether it will work in practice, exists already and be impactful.

The Patagonia group and trust, founded by Yvon Chouinard, is in every respect a societal company and knows it. Patagonia serves a diverse group of customers, with many products. What Patagonia has achieved in the clothing market, using profit to fund its non-profit purpose, is a signpost to what can be achieved across our economy through a societal sector. Yvon says "If we could do the right thing while making enough to pay the bills, we could influence customers and other businesses, and maybe change the system along the way".

The distinction between Patagonia and Motkraft, is that Motkraft's central societal purpose is not to increase profit to increase the resources available for social use, but to reduce profit to give customers a better deal. This is a different, but equally valid societal purpose.

Patagonia decided to "go purpose", in their own words, to help save our home planet, by fighting the environmental crisis, protecting nature and biodiversity, and supporting thriving communities. They are clear, they are a for profit business, impacting the world through its use of profit. Impact is determined by purpose and profit.

The option of selling Patagonia was not an appealing option for Yvon Chouinard, because the company could not be sure a new owner would maintain the company's values or keep their team of people employed.

Patagonia embrace two features of a societal enterprise. First, that the business needs to earn "enough to pay the bills", like Motkraft, profit need be only sufficient to meet its societal purpose and to sustain the business. Second, when the company prioritises keeping "our team around the world employed", they recognise that staff connect to purpose as stakeholders, for their personal well-being, rather than as factors of production whose cost should necessarily be minimised. Employment achieves the well-being for staff which arises from purposeful activity, one of the keys to personal happiness.

By connecting staff well-being to purpose through employment, Patagonia recognise the stakeholder interest staff should have in the enterprise economy. A Dutch supermarket, Jumbo, introduced low checkout lanes for lonely seniors wanting a chat, introduced as a part of the Dutch government's One Against Loneliness campaign. A Kletskassa, or 'chat checkout' was created and expanded because feedback was so encouraging, and 'chat corners' created where people could congregate for a refreshment and company. This connects customers well-being to purpose as stakeholders. It can be contrasted with the Amazon model for supermarkets, driven not by any societal purpose but to maximise shareholder value, by using technology to automatically calculate the value of shopping basket values when shoppers take goods from shelves, enabling them to reduce staff, leaving a barren shopping environment devoid of meaningful chatter.

The Patagonia trading company is a certified B Corp, benefit corporation, and its voting stock is held by the Patagonia Purpose Trust to protect its values. The trust owns 2% of the trading company and all the voting stock. The remaining 98% of the trading enterprise is owned by the Holdfast Collective, which uses the money it receives to further its environmental causes. The use of trust company structures is integral to the development of a societal sector. When Yvon Chouinard established this structure, he did so because there were no existing "good options available".

His declaration challenges the notion that we already have a suitable, established, and distinct corporate entity, which can give legal form to a societal sector. We do have benefit corporations, mutually owned companies, co-ops, non-profit and charitable organisations, but these are all rooted in ownership by shareholders, or members, or marginalised through their non-profit or charitable status. They are not trusts, or not structured to include them, as Yvon has, to ensure they operate purposefully throughout their existence, securing the profits they generate for the common good in perpetuity.

Had Yvon Chouinard not had the vision, or been less determined to go-purpose, then society would have lost the social and environmental benefits which will accrue in perpetuity over the life of Patagonia. Money is not bad, but the use of money determines its true value. Patagonia's use of profit will help protect the environment and maintain the "health and vitality of the natural world". It is that natural world, our place in it, and experience of it, which requires us to reset the dial in favour of purposeful enterprise.

Patagonia, like Motkraft, and so many other enterprises which fit into the societal model, prove that societal enterprises can be successful, able to transform outcomes, and shows a societal sector already exists. We need only to identify and develop it as such.

Government spending and debt

When there is a public spending review, or reference is made to "spending taxpayers' money", whose money is government spending, for what purpose and on behalf of whom?

At the end of the 19th century, average public expenditure was around 10% of GDP,[55] increasing to 41.3% in 2021.[56] Public sector debt exceeded GDP at the end of June 2023, the first time since 1961.

Something happened to our understanding of economy, public expenditure and debt following the industrial revolution, and the rise of free-market capitalism, counter-balanced by state intervention and its macro-economic management.

A person may earn sufficient income to finance increasing debt, yet as a level of debt is reached that may require stress-testing, the stress of that debt is likely to reduce their happiness. Our collective well-being deserves an answer to the same questions a person should ask in that situation:

- What is my debt being used for?
- Why is my debt increasing so?
- How is my well-being impacted by debt?

Is there an unspoken truth we must face up to: That we cannot finance the needs of society through low or historic rates of taxation and increasing debt. If debt is not the answer, then what is?

The advocates of a low tax economy, rely on levels of growth that may be hard to attain in a competitive, yet more protectionist global economy. Inevitably, spending financed by debt becomes the balancing and adjustable figure in the state's income and expenditure account, leading to austerity, unmet social need, or higher debt.

Public debt is used for many necessary social, and many unnecessary purposes, yet its primary one is to fill the gap left by insufficient taxation to finance government spending. Keynes identified the need to increase demand in the economy following the Great Depression, which started after a major fall in stock prices. In crisis, action was all, as it always is, and justified the Keynesian response. Unconsciously, Keynesianism moved responsibility for our collective well-being onto the state, who in turn passed it onto society, the only place where ultimate responsibility rests. The private sector demanded the best rate of return for shareholders, the lowest taxation and a monopoly over the market economy and got it; the result, society lost any rights to meaningfully share in the profits the market economy generates and to this day, must act as guarantors of ever rising debt to finance expenditure meeting social need.

The monopoly demanded by the private sector is so effectively embedded, that even though the private sector cannot deliver the social outcomes we require of it, we do not step in with a societally crafted solution.

Building a bridge between collectivist, societal need, welfare and values, and the capitalist economy has fallen on the state. This takes many forms. Norway does so through many state-owned enterprises, with the state owning shares in listed firms, controlling around a third of the total value of the Oslo stock exchange, with some where the goal is the highest possible return over time, and others owned for which government has various public policy goals.[57] Unlike the British government, which privatised BP in stages between 1979 and 1987, Norway invested in the North Sea through Statoil, now Equinor, formed in 2007 to merge Statoil with the oil and gas division of Norsk Hydro. It used surplus revenues from Statoil Norway to build up its investments into its sovereign wealth fund, estimated by the Economist magazine to be the largest of its kind in the world, becoming worth over $1 trillion in September 2017[58] and in May 2021 was estimated to be worth about $248,000 per Norwegian citizen. Norway's GDP per capita, the key measure of national individual economic prosperity, is double that of the UK and Norway is currently the second wealthiest country on Earth by this measure, while the UK comes in twentieth.[59]

The Norwegian model, influenced by social democracy, of state ownership for the common good, differs markedly from laissez-faire reliance on the private sector in the UK. The Norwegian government take on more responsibility for adhering society to the economy around shared economic interest. However, the Norwegian economy asserts collective rights through state ownership, not through opening-up the markets themselves to societal forms of enterprise. The Norwegian state intervenes to promote social and economic justice within the framework of a capitalist economy, not to propose an alternative to it.

China operates what is referred to as a socialist market economy, one in which a dominant state-owned sector exists in parallel with market capitalism and private ownership. Chinese market economics are described as socialist, yet the markets function as capitalist markets. Like Norway, prevailing political orthodoxy brings definition back to ownership and control.

In the UK our government has been pre-eminently Conservative, a party ideologically wedded to the supremacy of private share ownership. Paradoxically, the more government relies on laissez-faire capitalism, the greater the need for state spending to redress the inequity that arises from it. Our economic system and Keynesian response to it has hard-wired this paradox into our constant national discourse about competing demands over public spending.

Public expenditure has become the glue that holds society together, but it should be shared, unified purpose in a fair economic system that binds us.

For a significant part of the population, their disconnection from an economy which does not operate for their benefit alienates and disaffects. The problem is one of connection and rights, not just reallocated resource, and macro-economic management. The solution is to be found in the micro-world of economic forces, supply, demand, of consumer choice and an inclusive structure, representing broader stakeholder interests.

Equality, living standards and outcome are determined currently by the way profit and economic purpose attach to pre-existing capital. Equality, and empowerment, including gender, race and intergenerational empowerment depend on systemic reform of the market economy. If pre-existing wealth and producer interest does not determine outcome and rights, then what does? In a societal economy, it is consumers choosing to purchase from companies whose purposes they believe in, supported by governments elected on a mandate to build a fairer society, sponsoring the development of a societal sector.

Anecdotal reflection - Public expenditure – the societal lens. Nursing students.

Once upon a time student nurses served in work apprenticeships, paid for their work on the wards, often living together in accommodation provided by their hospitals. At the same time as universities were being expanded to take in many more students, the Project 2000 scheme elevated methods and procedures over knowledge and moved student nurses from the apprenticeship system at hospitals to being students of nursing, whose training was then contracted out to British Universities. Before long student nurses, were, like other students, taking on debt to pay their tuition fees and maintenance. A societal perspective of public expenditure requires us to look to the nature of expenditure and for the societal contribution that comes from it, in this case funding nurses. It is not simply a Treasury calculation of affordability and allocating scarce financial resource, essential as that is. Student nurses have not only paid for courses and paid their costs of living, often taking on debt to do so, they are obliged to work on the hospital wards, including on twelve-hour night shifts, throughout their training, for no pay. A societal response demands that we oppose such unfairness.

Capital, Debt, Funding and Enterprise

At the heart of our reliance on the shareholder owned company in the market economy is our dependency on share capital, which we attach to human values of personal ambition, enterprise, and individualism. The reality is that share capital, like debt, is just money. Share capital is money to which ownership rights are attached, debt is money with holding rights, related to a predetermined rate of return, interest.

If ownership through capital led to capitalism, what has finance through debt led to? If capital ownership, attached to corporate form, enhanced private claims to profit by diverting productive capacity towards personal enrichment, why has loan financing not led to the development of an enterprise economy which is not constructed around private share ownership?

The ownership of capital confers powerful rights of control, over profit, markets, goods, and people, including employees. Debt, like financial capital, is simply money resource, and like capital, confers power. However, it is potentially more hazardous. Capital gives a right to claim future profits in ways that can grow wealth and contribute to human progress, or can undermine society, but not necessarily so. Debt obligates borrower to lender for life, until debt is repaid, or default. For that reason, debt is permanent, and provided it is serviced by payment of interest lenders generally remain content; what else are they to do with their money other than to find new borrowers. At a macro-economic level, controlled, sustainable debt remains necessary and facilitates investment, improving our long-term growth potential. However, the dynamic of debt for the individual can be harmful, reducing living standards, well-being, the quality of lived experience and is potentially crippling. This is a societal issue. The power that creditors can assert over debtors, including national ones, shifts the balance of economic power, in favour of those that own over those in need.

We can become masters of our debt, and employ it usefully for our collective, enduring benefit. Capitalists attach share capital to profitable enterprise, for private gain through the limited liability, shareholder owned company. Society can attach debt to purposeful and profitable enterprise, for our personal and collective benefit through societal corporate form.

This is not complicated, it is simple, connecting the dots innovatively to societise the function of debt and make it work for our common good. Public, government debt, itself societally resourced, funds the activities of the state, and can also be used to finance the development of a societal sector. There is also a major role for the private sector and individuals, for those wishing to earn stable returns in a societal sector, at rates of interest reflecting commercial criteria, balancing risk and reward.

The main advantage for corporations issuing debt through bonds rather than shares is that ownership is not diluted, it is an alternative option for companies seeking to raise funds than issuing new share capital. In a societised sector, loan capital replaces share capital as the major source of corporate funding. The same factors determine its use: availability of funding, cost, and conditions attaching to loans, including reward. For retail investors in a societal sector, their returns will be significantly higher than those they have been offered by depositing savings with banks over many years.

Government borrows at the lowest prevailing rate, and will benchmark borrowing rates in a societal sector, as it does for all borrowing. Combined with a lower risk profile for the type of business most suited to societal form, the cost of capital in a societal sector should be low relative to that demanded by the private sector.

Private sector shareholders, often those most aggressively pursuing profit, have long realised the benefits and suitability of employing sustainably serviced loan finance as opposed to 'free' capital provided by shareholders; often for them a better option than using their own funds. The leveraged, private equity, buy-out is one such example. When the Glazers purchased Manchester United, they did so through a leveraged buy-out, borrowing £500 million from JP Morgan. A substantial portion of the loans to purchase the club, first formed as a railway works team in 1878, were payment in kind loans, on which interest could be paid by issuing further borrowing.[60] The payment in kind loans were subsequently sold to hedge funds. These funds are often investors in private equity funds.

If debt supporting private equity is considered a suitable method of finance to maximise privatised gains for shareholders, it can and should also be applied to fund societally purposed driven enterprises too.

Founding and Funding

There are established pools of finance, independent of government, which exist and could naturally be extended to support the development of a societal economy.

Capital supporting the development of a societal sector will be varied and exists already. Government sponsored debt capital, impact assessed and social sector investment capital including philanthropic sources of funding, retail investors seeking stable, secure returns, banks and private capital committed to societal purpose can contribute to the funding needs of a societal sector. Pension funds are also important.

Pension funds exhibit many societal characteristics, serving members interests, but whose members comprise general populations or groups within them. The societal framework exists to serve the best interest of this same population. A societal sector allows pension fund managers to broaden the horizons of their investment responsibilities, using the money invested by their members to improve outcomes their members experience during their working lives and to benefit wider society, through the societally purposed, well-being impacts the sector is designed to deliver. Even small, organic steps on the pathway towards a societal economy can improve lives in meaningful ways and pension funds are ideally structured and placed to support its growth.

Impact Investment, linked to sustainability and impact, aligns investor's values with their choice of investments, aiming to deliver investment returns alongside a positive impact on society. This recognises the increasing relevance of non-profit objectives for stakeholders in the economy. The elevation of impact investment criteria covering economic and societal challenges, including climate change, inclusion, health, well-being, and responsible and sustainable consumption validates a societal economic framework. The scale of this increasing market is evidence of the power of societal consumerism, and of investors demanding non-profit outcomes be achieved.

The Patagonia group is a for-profit, societally purposed company because it has built up its capital base through years of profitable trading. This gave Yvon Chouinard the ability to structure his company in accordance with his own ethical, values-based beliefs. Were Patagonia being formed today, as a start-up, operating within the same ethical framework, where would the company get its funding? We need a social funding model and capital institutions, sponsored by governments supporting a reformist programme, which funds the development of for-profit enterprises serving societal purpose, with performance measured both by profit and non-profit impact criteria.

Walking down Lamb's Conduit Street, I stopped to have a coffee at Redemption Roasters, a social impact assessed enterprise providing a pathway and training for offenders in prisons and helping them build a life outside. A little further on I discovered The People's Supermarket, "for the people, by the people", serving community minded ethical customers with fresh groceries that are in season. My impression was that this food store was under-capitalised, surviving, meeting the need of customers who wished to virtue spend but under-resourced. This is not the fault of the business model, but of the marginalisation it may face because we lack the sources of funding to build such a business into an enterprise of sectoral significance.

A societal market-economy offers the social investment community an opportunity to innovate, finance change and build-better. It requires their ambition, determination, and vision, to develop capital markets and processes underpinning a societal sector. Social funders can plot a course, to create social capital markets which are as effective for their purposes, as the private capital markets are in supporting the private sector. The vigour and energy this will take cannot be underestimated, nor can its importance to the development of a societal sector.

Stakeholders, Purpose, and Vision

Stakeholder interests are paramount.

In train travel, personal and collective self-interest converge if purpose includes offering best service, at lowest sustainable prices, through a national rail network.

The water industry provides water for household use, but we have a collective interest in having rivers which remain unpolluted by the discharge of sewage, by not having aquifers over used so that rivers' ecosystems remain vibrant and that there is adequate investment in sewage treatment plants and reservoirs.

These interests would be met through societally purposed structures for the rail and water industries, utilities, keeping the best of regional competitiveness and service, but aligned with collective needs, with profits ploughed back to ensure adequate investment in infrastructure is maintained, not diluted by shareholder claims to 'distributable' profits.

In a societal sector, stakeholder rights concern everyone but shareholders. Funders must be paid interest, with founding capital attracting greater rewards attached to their initial loan investment, and directors and managers of societal enterprises must be personally incentivised, as they are in the private sector. However, beyond these operational attributes, corporate purpose attaches to consumers, employees, those in the supply chain and those with a particular interest in the social and societal objectives of the company.

The Better Business Act campaign aims to repurpose shareholder owned businesses, through legislation requiring businesses to consider the non-profit interests of stakeholders, other than shareholders. Reform focuses on s.172 of the Companies Act 2006. It is a counterpart to the British Academy's Future of the Corporation project, inspired by the view that capitalism can meet societal need if businesses have a moral compass fixed to their dashboard. In June 2021 the Institute of Directors were pleased to report that almost half their members questioned thought that companies should have a purpose to help solve problems in society.[61] The Institute is a self-selected sample group, whose members are arguably more likely to appreciate the need for reform, making it more remarkable that despite nine out of ten having mission statements, half of those directors could not see a corporate purpose beyond shareholder interest.

The debate around s.172, can be seen in a wider, more revealing context. The Companies Act embeds the power which flows from member ownership. Irrespective of what other stakeholder interests it requires directors to have, under the heading, 'Duty to promote the success of a company', s.172 (1), a director "must act….. to promote the success of the company for the benefit of its members". This overriding legal obligation, seemingly reasonable, marginalises values-based companies, those operating for consumer and societal interest, not members' interests, to the outer reaches of our economy. Our legislative framework is fundamentally flawed in its scope because our economy is foundationally limited in its form.

This campaign, seeking what has been described as an "overdue change to the law that could save British capitalism" was reported the same week that the G7 proposed a "landmark" decision to agree a global minimum corporation tax rate of 15% to deter companies routing profits to tax havens.

Society may benefit if capitalism saves itself by defining purpose beyond shareholder interest, but ownership interest will always prevail in the private sector. It is an inherent characteristic of property rights which is the foundational attribute of market capitalism. It means a 15% tax take is considered "landmark", when society needs an answer to the obvious question, "what about the other 85%"? It explains why we suffer increasing debt, and social need remains unmet. Private sector capitalism, no matter how it is reformed, is not purposed to meet and fund a modern society and state.

As part of their plan to bail-out private sector banks, and to support the financial system from catastrophic meltdown following the 2008 financial crisis, the Treasury nationalised the Royal Bank of Scotland. In 2008 it made £ 20 billion of capital available to RBS, and following a second bailout in December 2009 the total was taken to £ 46 billion. The public ended up owning 84% of the bank. It was assumed that the natural passage for the RBS was to be returned to the private sector, but only once the bank, then nationalised, agreed to pay a fine imposed on it by US regulators for selling toxic mortgage bonds in the run-up to the financial crisis when privately owned. These penalties were applied even though governments were primarily at fault for neither regulating, nor supervising the financial markets properly and protecting the public, the most basic requirement of good government, in the run up to the 2008 crisis.

Having cleaned up the losses the bank suffered, used public funds to strengthen its balance sheet and seen the share price plummet following the crisis, the government had planned to sell the entire stake in Nat West, formerly

RBS, by 2023-24 at a projected loss to the Treasury of £ 38.8 billion. After the third sell-down of 'taxpayer-owned' shares, the public still hold 59.8% of the company with a deadline to sell the remaining stake by March 2025.

What was missing in the Nat West bail-out was any consideration of how it might be re-purposed, to challenge existing banking practices, outcomes and environment. A great opportunity has been lost, without a murmur of disapproval, because Nat West was not purposed beyond a shareholder framework; we do not conceive of collective rights in a societally purposed market economy.

Nat West is often referred to as being "taxpayer owned" but we must be careful, for which group of taxpayers are we referring to, those paying employee taxes or consumers paying taxes on sales through VAT, or businesses paying tax on their corporate profits? Nat West is public or societally owned, not "taxpayer" owned, because we all pay sales taxes, and those who do not pay direct employment taxes are still part of our community with rights to benefit from mainstream business activity. In 2014-15 some 31 million adults in the UK paid income tax, with 43% not earning enough to pay income tax. Total government receipts totalled £ 723 billion during the financial year ended March 2021 with £ 495 billion raised from generalised consumer and employment taxes and approximately a fifth of that, £104 billion from business rates, production, and corporation taxes.[62]

What the nationalisation of the bank illustrates is, that where there is a governmental will, there is a way;

corporate form is no obstacle to access public funds when the private sector needs them. Societal corporate form should not be denied us when it can be a conduit for the use of public funds to benefit the common good and address social need.

In an age when capital can be used to privatise the gains to be enjoyed from technological development, replacing labour in the process, it is imperative that the public is protected through societal, direct investment in the economy. This is more important than ever as we enter the age of AI. The issues concerning AI and technological development in our current age, are familiar from previous ones; a concern for adverse impacts on society and how development which can yield progress achieves socially acceptable outcomes. It is not technology which is necessarily harmful but the powerful link between the capital funding of its development, the ownership of its resource and the ethical standpoint of those providing the capital which distorts its potential for harm.

A private sector, demanding the highest return for more risky investment, owning the AI infrastructure, regulated by often powerless governments or governments who are motivated to use it for statist purposes, poses a risk to general well-being. The outcomes deriving from who benefits from the wealth technology creates, including AI, and who might be potentially harmed by its use, is connected to the greater issue of how power is exercised more generally through the market economy and by governments. This risk is heightened by the link between those who hold economic power and those who have power of governance, often self-serving and interconnected to one another. This power dynamic reflects our economy. A general population denied societal human and economic rights is vulnerable to the imposition of outcomes by those with power. It justifies repeating, that this is true in the matter of economics, just as it is in that of war or other human crises.

If we fail to societise the economy there will be increasing levels of inequality, with fewer people exercising increasing power over more of the population. It remains as ever, an issue of political, economic, and social justice.

* * *

What is our purpose, not of corporate purpose but our human, societal, social, and economic purpose? These purposes should be cohesive, one serving the other. A successful economy is not necessarily one that grows productivity and wealth, though this should be a principal aim of our personal and collective economic endeavour. It should be one which maximises human purpose and well-being, one that delivers societal health.

It is simple in an economy measured by numbers for us to place emphasis on data, where increasing numbers are generally good and decreasing one's bad. Measures of financial performance are important, but so are those of societal contribution and well-being.

We seek binary definitions, it makes classification easy; right or left, capitalist or socialist, agree or disagree, right or wrong, good or bad. However, human beings are more complicated, nuanced and spectrum. A binary definition of gender has been challenged and it is now generally accepted that we exist on a broad rainbow of gender identification. We define our economy in binary terms too; "business or government", "public or private". In the matter of profit, "for-profit" or "not-for-profit". This has arisen because we see profit as producer related, accruing to investors, it is the central, foundational feature of the private sector economy. Profit is the measure of performance, success, and reward in the private sector. It makes our economy ill-suited to modern society, unfit for many purposes. Deterministic definitions affecting our appreciation of economy need to be restated and profit is top of the list.

The reality is that markets exist and work, that governments have economic power, and there is a primary place for enterprise motivated predominantly by personal, private self-interest. Free markets are the rail tracks along which our economy travels, and are neither good nor bad, but the enterprises which currently serve them limit the good that society can extract from them. We can conceive a system which co-exists with the private sector economy, but directly challenges it, which embraces market forces and economics, and that fosters the entrepreneurial spirit and the profit motive, yet asserts collective rights over the economy. Market societism is that system.

Chapter 6

And so?

Our history, our past, and legacy enriches who we are, rewards us and haunts us collectively. We inhabit a political landscape and live in an economic system not of our making but conceived by others, for some this serves them well, others not.

The forces that shape who we become are genetic, values, systems and fears passed down through the generations and through nurture, our lived experience, affected by our environment and others, those who govern, assert authority over us, most important who we share society with. The same forces which determine our individual self are experienced collectively and determine the political and economic system we live under, which in turn affects economic and social outcomes, a behavioural and experiential loop which determines our lived experience.

We adapt our behaviour and develop as adults often unconscious of the reasons why we become who we are, behave, feel, and react as we do. This is the human condition. However, if trauma intervenes adaptive process can be prevented, the options of self can become diminished, we are who we have been told, or tell ourselves, we should be, not who we could be.

The same is true of our collective self, and the determination of our politics, economic system, and society.

The foundational strands of DNA that are carried into our current economy and body politic were those of hierarchy and through hierarchical status, ownership, of property and resource. This brought privilege, including opportunities to enjoy private gain through the exercise of power and control, over land and peoples. Militarism became a tool of state to assert economic power.

The shareholder owned, limited liability company has been used to attach the property rights of those with pre-existing capital and wealth to the profits the market economy generates. This is market capitalism.

Market capitalism could only develop in a democratic vacuum, when there was no gender, race or social class empowerment, few rights, and no universal franchise. Had these rights, now considered natural in modern society, existed two hundred years ago, demands for common law rights, under which every person is considered equal under the common law, might have been extended to include rights of equality over the economy.

The capitalist model of economy, forged in the furnaces of the UK's industrial revolution, is productive, profitable, able to serve the growth of the economy, yet is divisive and exploitative.

With no conception of universal societal right to inform the way our economy and politics might adapt, it was natural, perhaps inevitable that capitalism, by then symbiotically attached to Conservatism in the UK, would be opposed by an alternative philosophy rooted in power through ownership and control, only this time not by shareholders but by the state. Informed by Marx's ideas and observations about politics and economy, and the conditions of the working class, state ownership and control became the system of choice for those who opposed capitalism, and experienced or observed its inherent, intrinsic flaws.

The trauma of the first and second world wars, the 1929 financial crash and its aftermath, the Great depression, followed by the existential threat of the cold war halted any possibility of gradual, civilising reform as society evolved.

The reaction to the 1929 financial crash, a product of speculative investment systemically inherent in capitalism, most recently evidenced on a global scale in 2008, led to a contraction in credit and demand leading to the Great Depression. Private investors enjoyed the gains when times were good, some suffered when the market turned against them, but society bore the cost, through deprivation, unemployment, hunger, and early death.

It also led to a great political and economic paradox. The state, acting for the public good, stepped in to support the economy. Keynesian economic theory justified the intervention of the state to increase aggregate demand in the economy, through government expenditure and lower taxes, to encourage higher investment leading to fuller employment and a return to a stable economic environment.

The state became increasingly responsible for sustaining social cohesion, and a level of fairness inherently absent in capitalism, by macro-managing the economy through taxation, spending, and redistribution. This continues to divert attention away from reform of the distributive economy. The state committed its public, society, to an increasing burden of public debt to deal with the consequences of capitalism's limitations, leveraging risk away from the private sector, and passing it onto the general population. The paradox remains that state intervention remains an anathema for the advocates of the purest form of laissez-faire capitalism, but without it, capitalism's fundamental flaws would expose the monopoly it enjoys in the market economy to an existential, reformist threat.

Individualism, a defining feature of capitalism, has led to a society which elevates rights flowing from meritocracy, exceptionalism and equates equality with opportunity, rather than outcome. Yet it is outcomes, not opportunity, which determines well-being, through rights attached to our commonality.

Our system has become fixed in a current paradigm, a framework of ideas into which we try to fit policy, even though we fail constantly to deliver the outcomes we seek. Thomas Kuhn observed that paradigms are difficult to shift, and change will be resisted. Plato too, observed that we adhere to fixed systems and resist change necessary to bring about greater equality. The societal economy is a pathway to a new economic framework, and part of a paradigm debate.

Liberalism was marginalised by the competing claims for ownership of the economy, by private enterprise or state. Conservatism, authentic in its identity and self-certain of its authority, had for many decades, by the turn of the 19th century, been symbiotically attached to capitalism. Labour, through Clause 4 of its constitution committed itself to the common ownership of the means of production, distribution, and exchange, of industrial control. More than a century later the Liberal Democrats remain a party of values in need of an ideology. The Labour Party is in constant crisis because it has failed to reconcile its socialist heritage, with an ideology connecting it to the market economy. Both parties could rise to the challenge of reconfiguring our economy in favour of justice and fairness, but both may struggle to do so, even though they are both societally oriented. If neither of these two opposition parties take on responsibility for actively representing society, and its collective interest in the economy, then perhaps it will fall to a third, centrist, yet radical party, to emerge, and do so.

The Green Party's values and philosophy, of societal best interest, and a sustainable, sufficient economy fostering well-being urge us towards systemic societal change. The party which has done so much to save humanity and life on our planet from human inspired environmental degradation, arising from the same economic forces which affect our general economic well-being, is a societal one, subsumed under its green identity.

Political endeavour and support for societal reform, including societising the economy for the common good, is essential if systemic change is to be achieved. It is one element of an interconnected triptych of politics, ideology, and economics. If the ideology of societal, common good, of societism, foundationally supports the politics of society, its welfare, then it means little, unless it adheres to a unique, ubiquitous economic system which delivers well-being outcomes for the general population. Such a system must be credible, realisable, and offer certainty, unifying economic and societal purpose.

A societal perspective encourages us to challenge preconceived notions of economy.

Free market profits should be 'owned' by consumers as much as by producers. It is simply a question of purpose and corporate form. If the shareholder owned company gives producers access to markets for private gain, then the general population deserve a form of company that gives them, as consumers, and by extension society, rights over profits, for their personal and collective benefit.

It is said that alternative forms of enterprise, other than the shareholder owned company, exist. However, whether public benefit corporations, social purpose driven enterprises, or indeed for-profit social enterprises, companies owned as co-operatives, by employees or by guarantee, they fail to fulfil the role of providing a ubiquitous alternative to the shareholder owned company. These companies are often shareholder or member owned, and governed by members interests which does not guarantee societally purposeful outcomes in perpetuity. They are often compromised by their charitable status, trading as non-profit social enterprises, and are ill equipped to be the vehicles of reformation in the market economy.

The diversity of non-profit corporate form is a strength, but also a systemic weakness. The values of societal good need to attach to a distinct, societal entity connected to the for-profit economy, just as capitalism adheres itself to the shareholder owned company. This can be identified as the perpetual trust company, though a societal sector embraces social, not-for profit enterprises, and includes member owned companies working for social purposes across its broad range. That broad range covers the profit spectrum from non-profit, social enterprise at one end, through to the point where shareholder interest determines purpose and outcome at the other end of the spectrum.

In a game of societal catch up, there is a movement to refocus corporate purpose away from the primacy of profit towards social and non-profit purpose, by introducing a moral compass to guide private sector capitalism into less dangerous waters. This widespread movement has admirable aims, responding to the existential threat that capitalism poses to itself if it alienates society, but its impact will not introduce systemic change. The call from private equity, and shareholders in public companies, and measures of performance and value, demand that profit and capital value is maximised, even though some may see purpose beyond profit. This is the capitalist dynamic, the reason for shareholder owned companies existing, to make and distribute profit to business owners for their private benefit. The private sector continues to achieve much that benefits us all, including employment, productive growth, revenue for government, technological and scientific development, and above all meeting the demand of consumers for goods and services. It will remain the primary sector in our market economy, however it should not enjoy a monopoly status in the market economy.

The politics of societal rights, including economic ones, concern economic justice, fairness and our collective, common good. It demands the systemic recognition of values which impact on our well-being. An economy that is driven by private gain and exceptionalism does not respect the wonderful averageness of our humanity, the bell curve, which is universal, natural, imposed on us by brain power, lifespan, and our physical bodies. Our current market economy and the values that capitalism imbues are individualistic, of exceptionalism to grow personal wealth, often beyond reason. Societism is a philosophy rooted in increasing general well-being, and personal and collective wealth, based on our commonality and mutual interdependence.

Commonality of values for our collective good and shared purpose, including in our economy, speaks to the issue of not only what makes us wealthy but also healthy, maximising our well-being. Lord Layard, the Action for Happiness movement he helped establish and the NHS encourage us to think beyond absolute financial wealth. Kate Raworth's doughnut economics model helps us visualise a significant, new environmental paradigm. The economic expression, and counterpart of the well-being movement, which gives form to the doughnut, is the societal economy. It embodies and realises the principles of human endeavour which promote happiness, through connection, goals beyond self, and looking for what is good, being part of community, of society.

The most basic human right of the living is the right to life, from which all other rights flow. This takes us to the heart of the societist agenda for reform. Societal economics asks us to value that which is unquantifiable, the value one can place on the miracle of individual human existence and lived experience. This is a deeply personal matter, applies to us all, and each of us has a unique way of determining and responding to the existential evaluation it provokes.

Our economic system likes us to value products, services, resource and even lives, often by reference to its resource value or the value of resources that can be obtained by human displacement. Can we value a life? If we ignore Big Bang, the improbability of a life sustaining planet evolving to support us and focus on the reduced odds of us being born as the person we are, in that shape and form we are, taking how big the population is, it has been suggested that the chances of a person being born is one in four hundred trillion.[63] Dr Ali Binazir examined this figure and likened the odds of being born to 2.5 million people getting together, each playing a game of dice with trillion-sided dice, and each player coming up with the exact same number, say 550,343,279,001.[64] We simply cannot value life, it is priceless, of a magnitude beyond imagination, and this should inform our notion of economy and politics. Our economic system, and the corporate and national self-interest it provokes, diminishes humanity in favour of economic productivity, growth, and national power. It is important that people and societies thrive and flourish as a biproduct of economic prosperity, but not that others well-being is diminished to achieve it.

We are complex beings. We are not defined by singular and linear desires or expectation. It is perfectly reasonable for us to embrace capitalism, maximising our standard of living through endeavour and reward in a shareholder owned economy, whilst at the same time wishing to see other, common benefits accrue to ourselves, and those around us, helping those we know and care about.

The politics of change will determine how we live. If there is a philosophy for the common good which respects the significance of individual rights and freedoms, and we can envisage a societal economy operating for the common good alongside one inspired by capitalism, and the role of state, will our existing political parties deliver reform? This is a critical issue.

Without political will and action, little systemic change can occur, perhaps there may be some societal enterprise, but systemic reform and societisation rely on political engagement. Any of the parties in the UK can weave threads of a societal best-interest policy into their programmes and ideology. However, experience teaches us that it is difficult to embed foundational reform through existing institutions, which carry their own establishment heritable baggage, philosophy and world view tethering them to the past.

The radical politics and economics of societism may yet depend on the oxygen new generations can give it, and their connection with the politics of expectation, reform, and change.

The fellowship of reformers and those seeking greater economic justice need to coalesce, whatever their differences in opinion, diagnosis, and prescription, around a ubiquitous, unique, and identifiably new model of economy, a landscape that will nurture their ideas. If we fail to do this, then our ideas will be like seeds scattered in the wind. Systemic stasis for many is no bad thing, things carry on as ever, ideas come and go, debates and discussions continue, our world turns, but perhaps we need to step back and ask, is this enough, or do we need to seek fundamental reform and if so, what? This is not economic management, it is foundational change in favour of society, building the solidarity which flows from an economic system with intrinsic social expectation.

There is one group who hold all the keys, to power and reform, who can dictate the nature of our society, its values, and the way the economy functions, who can determine the fundamental question, who owns the economy and for whose benefit it operates? That group is society itself, the collective voice that we have, together, individuals demanding rights for unified purpose. That individual is you.

New horizons, a vision of a nurturing landscape, of a country the young want to inhabit, one fit for the modern age, can inspire paradigm change. Those who are older must help the young, for we are bound as generations, past and present, part of a society, sharing a personal and collective responsibility towards one another for our needs, security, and happiness. We are all of us individuals, living together, mutually dependent on one another. It defines our lived experience, who we are and our well-being.

To imagine a field of marigolds in bloom, in fertile soil, with a river flowing through it, where every bend presents a new vista, is to visualise an economic landscape where the best is maintained, but reform reshapes and improves it. An economy driven by societal purpose is one in which our national wealth is shared more fairly, through an extension of individual and collective societal rights. It promotes the well-being of the group, identified as our society, without sacrificing the significance of the individual. A better future demands a more just economy, responsive politics, and unified society. Civilising human progress, improving lives, is founded on universal values elevating principles of economic justice for the common good.

MY PERSONAL STATEMENT OF VALUES AND RIGHTS

I am an individual with human, social and economic rights. I am significant and have my own personal beliefs and values. I live in society, mutually dependent on others, benefiting from their activity, and accept obligations which promote our collective well-being and happiness. My lived experience is determined by me, my social and economic environment, and my relationship with those I am bound to in society.

I have a right to freedom of action and liberty, to pursue my own self-interest, provided it does not offend the well-being of others. I believe the society of which I am part should operate for my benefit, and collectively, that of my fellow citizens, based on virtues of care, fellowship, support, fairness and reasonable equality of outcome and opportunity.

We live with diversity, of beliefs, circumstance, outlook, and person. We may not be owners of capital, we may not rely on the State, but we are all members of society, interacting within home and community, with family, neighbours, as employers, employees, and as consumers, sharing our world's resources and environment.

Economy, reflecting societal diversity should be one operating for my personal benefit, but also for the common good, informed by collective, societal, political, and economic rights.

Society is a distinct economic entity, adhering to a unique and separately identifiable system of enterprise economy, of for-profit activity, but operating for societal purpose rather than returning profit to shareholders. Government should be always guided by societal best interest.

Reciprocity demands political representation. Society supports government, the function of state, borrowing and expenditure. Society underwrites the private sector, and bears the costs, human, financial and social burdens of its failures. There is no State without society, there is no business without consumers. Economic and social societal rights elevating the principle that we are all equal under the economy, as we are before the law, mandates systemic economic reform for the common good, leading to greater economic fairness and justice.

Societal well-being, rests on unified purpose, relationship, good health, and social cohesion, on respect for the values of self, but beyond self on universal values promoting human welfare, environment, and sustainable, healthy living. Societal values are not built on power and control, but human and humane virtues promoting the common good, well-being, happiness, and better quality of life.

Appendix 1

An artistic tribute

Too often we equate equality of rights with electoral franchise, when opportunity, expectation, and outcome is determined by landscape and environment. A universal electoral franchise requires economic franchise. Political democracy is incompatible with economic shareholder group autocracy, or oligarchy. A right to vote, too often condemns those without power, or the social and economically marginalised, those who do not excel or reap the benefits of mainstream economic activity, to quiescence, to be side-lined without an effective political voice. This is a place where minority rights are diminished, as indeed are rights attaching to the majority when only a minority are positioned to enjoy them. It is a place where race, gender and social injustice can build and endure. However, those who suffer this social injustice have the most powerful and significant voice, born of their experience, to demand reform.

One cannot fully appreciate the structural nature of discriminatory injustice which persists, nor the explosion of possibilities which arise in a reformed economy, without acknowledging the role of race and gender discrimination during the evolution of the economy, particularly arising from slavery, colonisation, and men's power over women. Its legacy hard-wires inequality into our society today. There is a connection between social, racial, and gender injustice, and discriminatory, economic marginalisation. This makes the demand for societal economic reform one of racial and gender equality too, and economic reformists, need the power of social movements such as those inspired by Me Too and Black Lives Matters to engage with this cause.

Art and poetry can inspire, revealing truths. Connections once made compel action.

In 2020 the BBC ran a series of film dramas under the title Small Axe, described as "love letters to black resilience and triumph in London's West Indian community" from the 1960s to 1980s, directed by Steve McQueen, who won a Best Picture Oscar for his film 12 Years a Slave. He subsequently made, with James Rogan, a series of three programmes examining a fire in New Cross in January 1981 which killed thirteen black teenagers, a Black People's Day of Action in March of that year, and the Brixton riots which followed in April, called Uprising. The series was, as described, vivid and visceral, depicting an experience of community wide discrimination, alienation, and brutality, suffered at the hands of the police, action justified by the government of the time. Forty years after these events, David Harewood, the actor, asked the question, "why is Covid killing people of colour", taking us back to systemic issues around race and social and health outcomes, often related to economic disadvantage. This is a compelling dramatic arc, linking colonisation, slavery, prejudice in London fifty years ago, and covid related health outcomes; over a period of less than two hundred years.

This is a relatively short period of time, dating from the depths of the Victorian industrial revolution when Marx and Engels were writing major works, to the current day. Marx wrote of "the effect the Chinese revolution seems likely to exercise upon the civilised world. It may seem strange, and a very paradoxical assertion that the next uprising of the people of Europe, and their next movement for republican freedom and an economy of Government, may depend more probably on what is now passing in the Celestial Empire – the very opposite of Europe – than on any other political cause that now exists".[65] He writes further in that year, 1853, "Whereas we say to the workers: 'You will have to go through 15, 20, 50 years of civil wars and national struggles not only to bring about a change in society but also to change yourselves, and prepare yourselves for the exercise of political power', you say on the contrary: 'Either we seize power at once, or else we might as well just take to our beds."[66]

Marx suggests it might take fifty years to achieve societal change during an enduring struggle and revolution for workers' power. However, he did not have a crystal ball, and we are still waiting for fundamental economic reform leading to societal change. His reference to China is not to the one we know today, a hybrid communist state embracing capitalism, but nevertheless China remains a catalyst for change. As he wrote, change begins within ourselves, an issue of consciousness and awareness.

The BLM and MeToo movements exemplify group solidarity in search of change. It is that solidarity which is needed in the matter of economic reform too.

Reform, not revolution, is now possible, not through force of arms but societal expectation and consumer rights attached to a societal economy. This societal economy is one which can be rooted in non-discriminatory outcomes and opportunity. It is one that challenges the foundational attributes of a discriminatory economic system. It is understandable that some people may want to pull down the statues of those who promoted slavery, but this is no more than a tickle on the heel of history, and we must be careful not to be satisfied with expunging the totems which remind us of the past, rather than understanding its legacy, compelling us to redefine the present.

That year, 1853, when Marx was writing on societal change and China, fits into our dramatic arc because that was the year Solomon Northup wrote and published his slave memoir, Twelve Years a Slave, on which Steve McQueen's film is based. Solomon was a free-born, African American New Yorker, kidnapped and sold into slavery in 1841.

The dramas we witness during the one-hundred-and-seventy-year period, since 1853 to the current day, from Solomon Northup and Marx to the Small Axe dramas, are profound, because they concern real lives, and lived experiences.

Engels, wrote his German text, 'The Conditions of the Working Class in England', observing the poor health, high death rate and the poor living conditions of labourers employed in Manchester between 1842 and 1844. The book was first translated into English in 1885 and published in London in 1891. It is no co-incidence that slavery persisted and that workers suffered deprivation too during this period, both products of the foundational attributes of capitalism. We have moved on to a post-Marxist, post-socialist economic world, arguably free from race slavery, though not all forms of slavery. However, our system of economy has not been fundamentally altered, and is still governed by the same systemic foundational ambitions for personal enrichment above societal good.

In the final scene of Steve McQueen and the BBC's Uprising series, we were taken to Fordham Park. In that park there is a monument to those young people who lost their lives on 18th January 1981 and as we reflected, Linton Kwesi Johnson read his poem, 'Towards Closure':

"These totemic oaks
Once fragile saplings
Taking root in hostile soil
Now bear perennial witness
To spring's eternal song of hope".

What is this hostile soil? Hope endures, but the soil and landscape must at some time give abundance and nutrition.

During Molly Kleiman's 2013 spring tutorial at NYU Gallatin, Alissa Jacques, then a student, raised questions about landscape that go to the heart of the issue. She takes the following text from Toni Morrison's, The Bluest Eye, published fifty years ago, in 1970:

"I even think now that the land of the country was hostile to marigolds that year. This soil is bad for certain kinds of flowers. Certain seeds it will not nurture, certain fruit it will not bear, and when the land kills of its own volition we acquiesce and say the victim had no right to live".

Alissa writes that Morrison's text describes the negative effect an environment can have on self, for if the soil is bad certain flowers cannot grow, if the environment is hostile then people cannot survive. She poses the essential question we must all ask ourselves: "is it our responsibility to find soil that nourishes us.... And if so, how? Or rather, should we fight in the soil in which we were born? But then when the land kills us... did we have a right to live?

The context of this work is racial disempowerment, but its metaphor and response to it, can be applied also to the matter of economic reform, not least because a landscape which cultivates collective, common good, equitable economic fruit is one in which disadvantaged and discriminated groups have greater power, as members of society, and consumers making choices every day of their lives. It is a landscape of empowerment.

Should we live in a hostile land with hope, the one we were born into, knowing we may die, or reshape that

THE ACCIDENTAL SOCIETIST

landscape? Can anyone who can visualise a fairer and better society and economy do anything but never look back, as John Donne suggests, but by seeking change, as waters that kiss one bank and do kiss the next one, achieve purest change that is the "nursery Of music, joy, life and eternity". Universal values, eternal human ones, compel change, not by revolution and force, but by recognition and adoption.

Alissa's poetic response to Toni Morrison's text reads:

"They say you can't grow
This land is too barren.
The dirt is too cracked.
This rain is too toxic.

They say you won't grow
You have a limp in your walk.
You have a twang in your talk.

They say you shouldn't grow.
Because white-washed books have taught
Your black history as inferiority
As a power struggle that succeeded to remind you
Of the poverty you will become.

The land is too barren.

But if we can alter the way you grow
Trim you down and prune you into
Something "manageable"
Something we find "pretty"

If we force you to hate yourself
Will you finally crack under the pressure
And conform?

This land can be fertile if we beat hard enough.

With the twang in your talk
With the way that you walk
With the beauty of your face, you will grow.
Because unlike what you've been told,
You are powerful beyond measure
Your roots can persevere.

And you as a marigold will bloom
Unfolding your petals burning with beauty
Red and yellow
Orange and gold
Ready to boast to the world your colors.

And they will love you.[67]

Alissa's depiction of a hostile landscape which limits us can be applied to any marginalised, discriminated against, or systemically disadvantaged group. If we are trimmed and pruned then we will conform, acquiescing to a system of values with which we might profoundly disagree, because we are taught there is no alternative, but she points us to the future; the landscape of hope which Linton Kwesi Johnson speaks of, where saplings become great oaks. It is a land, including an economic landscape that can be fertile if we beat hard enough, demand societal rights leading to greater non-discriminatory power, equality, and justice.

Group solidarity is everything in the search for justice.

The artist can visualise and express themselves in ways that raise our sights above our current horizon. That part of our artistic community which can speak to the issue of equality and reform, of racial, gender and economic empowerment, can do so in ways that will cut-through. To these artists I offer a tribute, for their endeavour and insight, and invoke, "continue and do more", so that all those who have been taught through history that they cannot grow, do indeed bloom as marigolds, stand strong as oaks; this is a manifestation of our greatest universal virtues of justice, compassion and empathy.

Appendix 2

Celeste Byers' artwork –
'We Are American'

(created for the Amplifier Foundation's
Realising Democracy project)

The activists Celeste Byers has drawn in her artwork, We are American, are, from left to right, Richard Aoki, Dolores Huerta, Ella Baker, Grace Lee Boggs, Toni Morrison, Eleanor Roosevelt, Rosa Parks, Vishavjit Singh, Martin Luther King, Vito Russo, Linda Sarsour, Zitkala Sa, Cesar Chavez, Bayard Rustin, Haunani-Kay Trask, Gloria Steinem, and Larry Kramer.

Celeste created this poster for the Realising Democracy project.[68] Her illustration is "a celebration of the culturally diverse array of activists from (US) history. I chose to use the classic American symbols of the flag, the rose, and the bald eagle along with daisies which represent new beginnings". These symbols, often associated with conservatism should be "claimed as our own because this country is all of ours".

The activists in Celeste's illustration appear to move with collective purpose, occupying their own space, often looking to their own horizon, but their direction of travel is shared, to a destination, a land in which their values and aspirations for social progress are realised. This land is the same one which Alissa Jacques writes of, in which the weak and marginalised can be powerful beyond measure. The activists' causes are manifold, but all rooted in greater justice, through civil, human, and social rights, race, and gender equality. They share purpose but have experiential viewpoints determined by diverse ethnic heritage. They use their talents, as organisers, advocates, thinkers, poets, authors, dramatists, and as people on the front-line of their separate causes which unify around the concept of a more humane, fairer society, bonded through our commonality.

When Celeste, places classic American symbols like the eagle and flag in her artwork, "to claim them as our own", she visualises an eternal truth speaking to the essence of the systemic issue we face. This land, as Woody Guthrie sings, is your land, it is made for you and me; it should be, but is it? Like our symbols, this land exists for us all, and should be made for us to inhabit, but we can feel separate from it, be disconnected from the outcomes we expect in it, because, since time immemorial it has been designed for the greater benefit of some but not all. Our society has become defined by the politics and economics of difference, not our commonality. It is not "our land", yet, which is why it remains essential that activists continue to work and organise, and why those in Celeste's illustration are marching to a land in the distance. The daisies we can see in this new landscape herald the new beginnings to which Celeste refers, often seen as representing spring, new chapters in life, fresh and positive friendship, loyalty, purity, joy, and cheerfulness. This then is a land of hope.

Our society, the values we live by and through which we experience life, for good or ill, are determined by, and causally linked to an economy which is not "ours". This fosters the politics which become unrepresentative of the diverse values we hold, and worse still, embed the politics and control of power, diminishing our democracy and the rights of general populations, of societies across our planet.

The bridge we need to cross, to move from current lived experience to hope and the reality of a better future for the greater number of us is to be found in our understanding of the economy and linking our vision for reform to a new political and societal landscape. This new landscape is the collective framework which can nurture the social and human causes activism represents. The activist, reformist movement can achieve progress by unifying around a common purpose, whilst sustaining their separate, unique claims for reform and change. These are universal issues, which like our economy and the societies it determines, cross national boundaries. Celeste's artwork, directed to an American public, is of universal significance, and in its foundational values and aspirations will be shared with artists, thinkers and populations across all nations and societies, including those in the UK.

Celeste produced her artwork for the Stanford Social Innovation Review, as part of the Realising Democracy project, addressing underlying systemic roots of exclusion and inequality, funded by the Ford Foundation, an organisation committed to "building a world where everyone has the power to shape their lives". The project examines the roots of civil society, power and democracy that undermines "people's ability to create the world they want and deserve", advocating policy and organisational responses by choosing "a different, more inclusive path, one grounded in people-centred democracy and the nation's most deeply shared values".

Celeste's artwork accompanies a contribution on Reclaiming Civil Society, by Marshall Ganz and Art Reyes which recognises that society is "a vital source of autonomous power dependent neither on government nor on private wealth – but is capable of influencing both and that "organisers have a significant role in renewing democracy through the creation of an inclusive constituency". They quote Alexis De Tocqueville, in Democracy in America, describing "knowledge of how to combine", as the article's authors say, "to transform individual self-interests into common interests....... turning individual resources into collective power". The authors describe how firms we classify as non-profit are in reality accountable to high-net-worth individuals and foundations who fund them. The authors argue that the reformist movement is fractured and have not acquired what Tocqueville called "habits of the heart", micro practices that can turn motivation into the macro power needed to create real change. That, quoting the feminist sociologist Jo Freeman, the reformist movement and its organisers have fallen victim to the "tyranny of structurelessness".

A societal social framework exists, yet political and economic rights embedded into this framework, giving power as well as influence, should be our expectation, beyond philanthropy. Our organisational diversity is both a strength and our greatest weakness, leading to structurelessness. The "inclusive constituency" which can renew democracy exists but depends on us recognising it and that we personally commit to being a part of it. That constituency is "Society". The philosophical basis for this framework, flows not just from the knowledge of how to combine which Tocqueville speaks of, but a political movement and economic system which embodies the very characteristics to which he refers, which transforms individual self-interests into common ones by merging them. This philosophy is clear, it too exists, a societal one, a social and political philosophy that promotes the well-being of the group, of society, without sacrificing the significance of the individual.

Structure and power come by adhering this philosophy to its natural social and political constituency. However, to turn individual resources, values, into collective power requires a sector of the economy which recognises the reality of the economic world we live in, markets based, but challenges the presumption that those markets and the profits they generate cannot be societal too. This is the alternative to capitalism which can transform lives, given the individual, reformist, and collective political will to do so; this is market societism, an antidote to monopoly, market capitalism and the structures of power it relies on and embeds in society. This alternative produces well-being outcomes for society, collectively and individually through the power of political allegiance and consumer choice. Markets, and the economy which flow from it, can belong to the general population, to 'the people'.

The Realising Democracy project authors, Felicity Wong, K. Sabeel Rahman and Dorrian Warren contribute an article on Democratising the Economy making the links between public policy, economic inequality which breeds political inequality and a core economic problem that wealth and influence are concentrated at the top of society and business. This "civil oligarchy is heavily skewed by patterns of durable racial and gender inequalities". This is an inevitable consequence of the legacy we have inherited, of systems of power adhered to systems of economy which were introduced through colonisation, affecting the rights of groups represented in Celeste's artwork, and the diminished rights to self-determination of ethnic groups and societies across the globe, and communities within our nations. It affects the generalised cost of living and levels of well-being across the general population too; it is a systemic issue.

To realise a "truly inclusive democracy requires tackling (the) parallel problem of economic power", the authors call for a democratisation of economic power and lay down three challenges: to dismantle and rebalance the extreme concentration of power in the hands of a small number of corporate and financial firms, to use the power of government and civil society to ensure economic decisions reflect the full range of stakeholder interests and that communities must have more direct influence in the business of economic decision making. To break what they call the "neoliberal stranglehold" the writers suggest de-rigging the economy by creating a new policy agenda to shift economic power, building up the countervailing power of government and civil society and crafting institutional designs that democratise economic governance more broadly.

The analysis and policy responses are well founded. A societal perspective has a contribution to make to the interventionist, governance, and changes in public policy to which the authors aspire. However, it is proven beyond doubt that the economy operates beyond the power of government, that governance is unreliable, and that outcomes are determined by the way markets operate. Democracies fracture because the economy operates directly and inherently for self-interest above self-interest aligned to common purpose. Elected governments, the fulcrum of democracy, can oppose common rights and can benefit from polarising populations, utilising networks of power which diminish our ability to achieve, fair, equitable, well-being outcomes in society.

The reformist movement concede the ground, not just the neo-liberalist ground but the entirety of the land they wish to reach, which nurtures their social and human aims, not because they lack the power to bring about change, but because they do not use that power to ensure the market economy is democratised through a societal economy. This too exists, we only need to identify it, and develop its unique characteristics.

The land to which Celeste's activists march is one we can universally craft, in which we can plant our reformist seeds and know they will be nurtured, challenging centuries of embedded discrimination through empowering rights. We need to get political about it. This is a cause, yet we must always be humane and respectful of one another's differences, never forgetting the significance of the individual, whose greatest chance in life is to experience that life in the first place. To realise democracy, to live in the land Celeste asks us to visualise, is to raise the banner in solidarity for the social and political constituency that is Society, breathing in the refreshing air of societal reform, adhered to a societal economy. These are the new beginnings that can bring hope, a fairer economy, politics, and society.

Appendix 3

A localised diversion to Winterton-on-Sea

Our nation is comprised of communities, like that of Winterton, of people surviving and prospering through trade, but relying on mutual interdependence since time immemorial.

Walking along the coast from Winterton towards the Horsey Gap on the dunes, the wind off the North Sea usually blows strong. Seals pop their heads out of the water and peer at the people staring at them, sometimes to be seen as colonies sun-bathing on the beach. The female seals and pups occupy one part of the beach, the bull seals another, and people yet another. After several miles you can cut inland, across flat tracks and fields to Horsey Mill on the edge of Horsey Broad, to enter a landscape of water and fenland reeds. Throughout your journey, the Southern view is dominated by what would commonly be identified as Norman churches, particularly the one at Winterton, an imposing monument on the horizon. The dunes form part of a sea defence against ever changing sea levels, with most low-lying fenland

being no more than ten metres above sea level. The
light house on the coast at Winterton, now sits several
hundred metres from the sea on the landside bank of
Winterton Valley, a small depression between solid land
and the dunes. It replaced the original light, to guide
shipping, displayed from the tower of the Church.

There has been a church since Anglo-Saxon times, with a
parish having been created in 967. The early settlement
of farmers who were fishermen in the winter may have
given the village its name, referred to in the Domesday
Book, 1086, as Wintretona or Wintretuna. In fact, the
church one sees today, mostly dates to the 16th century.
The building would have been a powerful totem of
omnipresent power, of divine, godly presence on the one
hand, and church and feudal lordship on the other; an
everyday reminder not to transgress or challenge. The
same citadels have been built across our city scape in our
lifetimes, office blocks declaring the deity and supremacy
of the financial markets. Walk through the graveyard of
Winterton church, look around you, enter through the
South porch which doubles up as a community library
and you enter the lived-in church, one that becomes of
the people in their everyday lives.

The graveyard is occupied by Georges, Kings, Hodds
and Empsons. Empsons Loke, or small lane, runs
adjacent to the church. A fisherman's net hanging from
the North wall of the church, and the name of the
Fisherman's Return pub, are testament to the villager's
sea life. There is a memorial to those who died in the
world wars of the 20th century including two Kings in

each of those conflicts, fathers and sons, three Hodds and an Empson having also died during WW2. Slate plaques record those who served their community on lifeboats. The rectors of Winterton are recorded, including Walter de Clere in 1346. The de Clere's were descended from Richard Fitz Gilbert, Lord of Clare, a kinsman of William the Conqueror, who accompanied him during the Norman Conquest. As time marched on Walter was followed by Robert, Walter and William Clere less the Norman prefix, 'de'; dynastic power embedded in the community under the umbrella of church and state.

A glance at our physical landscape bears witness to the history we inhabit. It is largely fixed, gradually changing and forms the setting in which communities and individuals attempt to live their version of a best life. That life should be enhanced by an economy and politics which directly serves their personal, community and societal interest best.

Acknowledgements

I have received the unwavering support of my wife, Sarah, who has encouraged me to develop my ideas for societal reform, and to write this book, proofreading it and challenging my text.

During the development of my ideas I received encouragement from a range of commentators, academics, and politicians, who showed generosity of spirit, replying to letters, and engaging with my formative thoughts on the societal economy. Sir Vince Cable thought the use of the existing housing stock to create affordable homes to be exactly what is needed. Professor Diarmaid MacCulloch and Matthew Parris gave thoughtful responses, which suggested to me a societal perspective had meaning. It was Polly Toynbee who pointed out that the problem is "how to get such ideas out to a basically conservative country, that keeps voting for the opposite, against their own interests", which led me to think of societal best interest, in a societal sector, as a point where personal and collective self-interest converge. Martin Wolf made several useful, critical observations, and said he was open to persuasion, which fired me up with a belief that a paradigm debate was possible.

Sarah Ralphs read an early draft of the book. Sarah's belief that a societal system offered a different way of doing things, that she had given up hope but could see there was a way forward, made me determined to publish the book, and engage with reformists through a broad political process. Sarah and I co-founded the Society Alliance, a group campaigning for a societally purposed, democratised, and values-driven economy.

The poetry of Alissa Jacques and Celeste Byers' art inspired me, to search for a land fit for 'marigolds to bloom', where the marginalised are "powerful beyond measure", and to visualise new beginnings "because this country is all of ours".

I am grateful to those who have political allegiance yet have been willing to consider the societal pathway to a more just and fairer society, one which may challenge their institutional heritage.

Finally, I must acknowledge you, the reader, for giving up your time to engage with an issue of profound importance, that of economic justice, quality of life and well-being.

Works Cited

1. **Tillery, Gary.** The Philosophy of John Lennon. *Philosophy Now.* 2005, Issue no. 52.

2. **The Joseph Rowntree Foundation.** *Poverty and Ethnicity: A review of evidence.* May, 2011.

3. **Stroud, Baroness Phillipa.** Measuring Poverty 2019. 29th July 2019.

4. **Department for Work and Pensions.** Households below average income: an analysis of the income distribution, 1995 to 2020. 25th March 2021.

5. **Morrison, Toni.** The Bluest Eye. Published by: Rhinehart and Winston. 1970.

6. **The British Academy.** *Reforming Business in the 21st Century, para 1 of the Executive Summary.* 2018.

7. **Adebowale, Lord Victor.** Purposeful Business for an Inclusive and Sustainable Economy. *The British Academy, Future of the Corporation Project.* 4th February 2021.

8. **Fisher, Dr Naomi.** Just what makes us who we are? *The Psychologist.* 23rd January 2019.

9. **Plomin, R.** Blueprint: How DNA Makes Us Who We Are Published by Allen Lane. 2018.

10. **Maddox, L.** Blueprint: How Our Childhood Makes Us Who We Are Published by Little Brown. 2018.

11. **Weingast, Barry R.** Adam Smith's Theory of Violence and the Political Economics of Development. January, 2017.

12. **Rutherford, Janette, et al.** Who comprised the nation of shareholders? Gender and investment in Great Britain, c. 1870-1935. January, 2010.

13. **Daniels, Barbara.** Poverty and Families in the Victorian Era. March, 2003.

14. **Jacques, Alissa.** They say you can't grow. *NYU Gallatin.* May, 2013.

15. **Dictionary, Oxford English.**

16. **Common Good Foundation, Registered charity no. 1163668.** *Website.* See also: Leslie Deighton's series of 'little' books giving flesh to the idea of the common good.

17. **Allan Baker and Charlotte Fellows.** Life Expectancy in England in 2020 Published by Public Health England. 31 March 2021.

18. **Office for National Statistics.** *Health state life expectancies by national deprivation deciles, England: 2017 to 2019.* 22 March 2021.

19. **Written by Christopher McQuarrie. Director: Bryan Singer.** The Usual Suspects. Release date: January 25, 1995.

20. **Clarence-Smith, Louisa.** KPMG aims for a third of its staff to be working class. *The Times.* 9th September 2021.

21. **Social Mobility Commission.** *State of the Nation 2021, Social mobility and the pandemic.* July 2021.

22. **Layard, Richard.** Happiness: Lessons from a New Science Published by Penguin Books, 2005. 2005.

23. **Richard Layard, Sir Anthony Seldon, Geoff Mulgan and Mark Williamson.** *Action for Happiness.* Co-founded in 2010.

24. **Robert Kennedy.** *Speech at the University of Kansas.* 18th March 1968.

25. **World Economic Forum.** Davos Manisfesto 2020: The Universal Purpose of a Company in the Fourth Industrial Revolution. 2020.

26. **United Nations - Department of Economic and Social Affairs.** Transforming our world: the 2030 Agenda for Sustainable Deevelopment. April, 2018.

27. **Met Office.** Causes of climate change. *Website https://www.metoffice.gov.uk/weather/climate-change/what-is-climate-change.*

28. **You Gov poll Published by the Food Foundation.** 24.08.20 to 01.09.20.

29. **Commission on the future of social housing.** Building for our future: A vision for social housing. January, 2019.

30. **CPRE - The Countryside Charity.** Countryside next door: State of the Green Belt 2021. February, 2021.

31. **Halifax Building Society.** *The Halifax Buying vs Renting Review.* April, 2021.

32. **Office for National Statistics.** Office for National Statistics Report: UK private rented sector -2018. 18th January 2019.

33. **Davies, Rob.** Bet365 boss's £421m pay for 2020 takes earnings over £1bn in four years. *The Guardian.* 31 March 2021.

34. **ONS.** *Drug Misuse in England and Wales: Year ending JUne 2022.* December, 2022.

35. **Her Majesty's Inspectorate of Constabulary and Fire & Rescue Services.** *Disproportionate use of police powers - A spotlight on stop and search and the use of force.* February, 2021.

36. **Sentencing Council.** *Investigating the association between an offenders sex and ethnicity and the sentence imposed at the Crown Court for drug offences.* January, 2020.

37. **NHS.** *Hospital admissions for cannabis use - 2007-08 to 2016-17.* December, 2018.

38. **Dr Marta Di Forti and Others.** The Contribution of cannabis use to variation in the incidence of psychotic disorder across Europe. Lancet Psychiatry. March 19, 2019.

39. **Smith, Hannah Lucinda.** Albanian cannabis farmers get rich supplying Britain The Times. 9th August, 2019.

40. **ONS.** *Public sector finances, UK: March 2021.* 23 April 2021.

41. **Aldrick, Philip.** "Raising tax on business will kill off investment", CBI says. *The Times.* September 13. 2021.

42. **Bank of England.** *Monetary Policy Report.* August, 2021.

43. **Hurley, James.** Lessons for Taxpayers from 'favourite English teacher'. *The Times.* September 13, 2021.

44. **Donne, John.** *Poems of John Donne, Vol 1, E.K. Chambers ed.* London: Lawrence & Bullen, 1896. 106-107.

45. **Astra Zeneca.** *Annual Report and Chairman's Statement.* 2020.

46. **Paul Swinney - Centre for Cities.** Levelling up 'will cost as much as reuniting Germany'. *The Times Article written by Emma Yoemans.* August 16, 2021.

47. **Thatcher, Margaret.** ("No such thing as society") Interview for Womens Own. 1987.

48. **Bartlett, Thomas.** *Ireland – A History.* Cambridge : Cambridge Univeristy Press, 2010.

49. **The Green Party of the United States.** https://www. gp.org/economic_justice_and_sustainability_2016. [Online]

50. **gwleidyddiaeth.cymru.** Socialism in Welsh Politics. *https://www.gwleidyddiaeth.cymru/socialism-and-communism/socialism-in-welsh-politics/.* [Online] 2018.

51. **Schama, Simon.** A History of Britain. *The British Wars 1603–1776.* 2009. Published by The Bodley Head. London.

52. **Guthrie, Woody.** Song: This Land is Your Land. Published 1st September 1945. Recorded November 1944.

53. **Aldrick, Philip.** Low-paid workers are the biggest victims of modern monopolies. *The Times.* 6th July, 2021.

54. **McKInsey & Company.** *Private markets come of age. McKinsey Global Private markets Review 2019.* February 2019.

55. **Brien, Philip and Keep, Matthew.** The public finances: a historical overview House of Common Briefing Paper 22 March 2018.

56. **Clark, D.** Total public sector current expenditure as a share of GDP in the UK from 1977/78 to 2020/21. July 22nd, 2021.

57. **Norwegian Ministry of Trade and Fisheries.** New report to the Storting on state ownership. 22nd November 2019.

58. **The Economist.** Norway's sovereign-wealth fund passes the $1trm mark. *The Economist.* September 23rd, 2017.

59. **Smith, Nick.** North Sea Oil: A tale of two countries. *E&T, Engineering and Technology.* January 20, 2021.

60. **The Guardian.** Manchester United debt increases to £716.5m, lastest accounts confirm. *www. theguardian.com/football/2010/manchester-united-glazers-debt-ronaldo.* 20 Jan 2010.

61. **Institute of Directors.** IoD: 6 in 10 firms believe they should not exist solely to make money. 02 June 2021.

62. **Office for National Statistics.** *Public sector finances, UK: March 2021.* 23 April 2021.

63. **Robbins, Mel.** *Ted Talk, You are 1 in 400 trillion.* November 15th 2018.

64. **Binazir, Dr Ali.** Are you a Miracle? On the probability of you being Born. [Online] Huff Post contributor platform, August 16th 2011.

65. **Marx, Karl.** Revolution on China and In Europe. *New York Daily Tribune.* Articles on China, 1853–1860, June 14, 1853.

66. **Marx, Karl Revelations Concerning the Communist Trial in Cologne. 1853.**

67. **Jacques, Lisa. Confluence, For Certain Kinds of Flowers.** *NYU Gallatin, Confluence.* [Online] **May 10, 2013.**

68. *Stanford Social Innovation Review, Winter 2020.* **Realising Democracy Project, Various authors.**

9 781803 817842